James
Working Out
Your Faith

Bruce BICKEL
&
Stan JANTZ

HARVEST HOUSE PUBLISHERS

EUGENE, OREGON

Cover by Left Coast Design, Portland, Oregon

Cover photo © Steve Terrill, Portland, Oregon, www.terrillphoto.com

Bruce Bickel is published in association with the literary agency of Mark Sweeney & Associates, 28540 Altessa Way, Ste. 201, Bonita Springs, FL 34135

Stan Jantz is published in association with the literary agency of Mark Sweeney & Associates, 28540 Altessa Way, Ste. 201, Bonita Springs, FL 34135

CHRISTIANITY 101 is a registered trademark of Bruce Bickel and Stan Jantz. Harvest House Publishers, Inc., is the exclusive licensee of the federally registered trademark CHRISTIANITY 101.

JAMES: WORKING OUT YOUR FAITH
Copyright © 2008 by Bruce Bickel and Stan Jantz
Published by Harvest House Publishers
Eugene, Oregon 97402
www.harvesthousepublishers.com

Library of Congress Cataloging-in-Publication Data
    Bickel, Bruce, 1952-
    James : working out your faith / Bruce Bickel and Stan Jantz.
       p. cm. — (Christianity 101 Bible studies)
    ISBN-13: 978-0-7369-2294-4
    ISBN-10: 0-7369-2294-6
    1. Bible. N.T. James—Commentaries. 2. Bible. N.T. James—Study and teaching.
    I. Jantz, Stan, 1952- II. Title.
    BS2785.53.B53 2008
    227'.9107—dc22

                             2007046139

Contents

A Note from the Authors

*S*o, you're thinking about studying the Bible's book of James, eh? You've made an excellent choice for yourself, and we can say that even though we don't personally know you. We're confident in our assessment, however, because James is different from other books of the Bible and it provides a refreshing—and necessary—perspective on the Christian faith that you don't find emphasized with such clarity elsewhere in the Bible. So, James is a great book to study regardless of whether...

- *You recently became a follower of Christ, and you need some practical orientation about your newly adopted faith.* The book of James is the place to find it. You'll discover principles about dealing with problems and temptations. (You didn't think those would all go away when you became a Christian, did you? While some of the televangelists might make it seem otherwise, trials and tribulations are a regular part of a Christian's life, but James puts an interesting spin on them—we're told to rejoice in the midst of adversity because those circumstances give God an opportunity to work in our lives.) Other topics in James are less painful but equally relevant, such as controlling our gossip, handling our money, and using our time in a spiritually productive manner.

- *You've been a Christian for a while but the excitement has worn off, and you are anxious to revitalize your walk with Christ.* Does it seem like you are just going through the motions and have lost a real passion for Jesus Christ? Are you "playing the game" of Christianity but finding little fulfillment in your faith? Do you have an intellectual understanding of who God is but don't seem to be showing any connection to Him in your everyday life? If that is your condition, then you fit into the target audience to whom James was written.

- *Studying the Bible is something new for you.* Well, congratulations. One of the best ways to know God better is to read His Word. And the book of James is a great place to start. Studying the Bible can be intimidating, so you might want to ease into the process, favoring a practical approach rather than jumping headfirst into deep theological concepts. There is nothing wrong with the doctrinal complexity of Romans, or the prophetic imagery of Revelation, or the ancient cultural references of Leviticus. Those Bible books should definitely be on your study list. But James is a good place to start because it approaches Christianity from a real-life point of view. (Plus, it is only 108 verses long.)

- *You sometimes catch yourself wondering if you are really a Christian at all.* Do you call yourself a Christian but seem to have no real connection or relationship with God? Do you wonder if your faith is authentic or fraudulent? Wouldn't it be nice if there was some way to tell for sure? James won't give you a pass/

fail checklist, but you will find descriptions of the evidence and proof of a genuine Christian faith. James describes what the target looks like, and you can determine if you are making progress toward the goal.

We all can use a practical how-to manual from time to time, and James is just that for the Christian life.

Thinking Outside the Book

This Bible study is part of the Christianity 101® series, which includes other Bible studies and larger resource books (such as *Knowing the Bible 101* and *Knowing God 101*). All of these books are designed to present the truth about God in a manner that is correct, clear, and casual. We wrote the Bible studies to give you additional background information (like you'll find in a commentary, only not so technical), along with questions that encourage you to apply what you have studied to your personal life circumstances.

Because you were shrewd enough to purchase this book (or snatch it from someone else's backpack), you are invited to log onto the Web site at www.ConversantLife.com/101. There you will find additional resources, information, and questions that may be helpful in your study of James. (You might even be convicted about that backpack theft.) You can also use the Web site to e-mail us any questions you have about what you have studied. Look at the end of this book for more information about these online features. As you'll see, you can use the Web site to find supplemental, resources relating to all of the books in the Christianity 101® series.

If you've already flipped through the pages of this book, did you notice what was missing? This book is already 15 times longer than the book of James itself, so we didn't reprint all of those 108 verses. That's what your Bible is for. We suggest that you read the biblical text first, then read the corresponding chapter in this book, and then read the biblical text again. If we have done our job as commentators, then you should get more out of the text on your second reading.

This book is a supplement to your Bible, so if you only have time to read one of the two books, then read the real deal. What we have written will give you some good background information, but the better inspiration and instruction are found in James (despite claims from our mothers to the contrary).

At the end of every chapter, we've included questions. We've omitted the answers because we wanted to remove the temptation for you to cheat. Actually, there are no wrong answers because the questions are designed to promote personal reflection on the biblical text. If you are studying by yourself, you don't need to answer the questions out loud. If you are studying in a group, social courtesy suggests that you respond audibly.

Seeing If Your Faith Really Works

Because you are serious enough about your Christian faith to be studying the Bible, we are confident that you'll benefit from reading James. Perhaps more than any other New Testament book, you'll be challenged to examine the practical aspects of how your faith affects the way you live.

As we wrote this book, we prayed that God would guide our words to clearly communicate how James's instruction can help you examine the authenticity of your faith. But you should also know we've been praying for you, too. Really. We know your study of James will give you the occasion to consider whether your thoughts, expressions, and actions are consistent with your spiritual beliefs.

For James, the essence of his message was to challenge people to implement their faith in their everyday lives.

> *Do not merely listen to the word, and so deceive yourselves. Do what it says* (James 1:22 NIV).

James wanted his readers to move their faith from mere theory into purposeful living. And that is our prayer for you.

James says less about the Master than any other writer in the New Testament, but his speech is more like that of the Master than the speech of any of them.

—D.A. Hayes

$\mathcal{A}$ $\mathcal{S}$plit of $\mathcal{O}$pinion

With 66 books in the Bible, you would expect that some are considered more popular than others. Leviticus usually doesn't make the "favorites" list because it talks about sacrificial rites that involve dissecting the innards of a goat or sheep. And the writings of the so-called minor prophets (such as Habakkuk, Zephaniah, and Haggai) aren't often on anyone's "most loved" list—probably because no one feels confident pronouncing their names. And for the most part, people gravitate to the New Testament books instead of the Old Testament ones because they tell the stories of the life of Jesus (Matthew, Mark, Luke, and John), and the stories of the early church (Acts), and give lessons about God and the Christian life (the rest of the New Testament, with the exception of Revelation, which you read if you want to throw your brain into sensory overload).

But the readable and practical epistle of James, tucked away near the back of the New Testament, makes the short list for many people. So why has it received criticism, with its contribution to the Bible seemingly devalued—at least by one of the heavyweights of Christendom? It is almost as though the contribution of James in the Bible has been denigrated. Is this any way to treat a book of the Bible that might have been written by a half-brother of Jesus Christ Himself? What could stimulate such controversy? The answer to that question will sharpen your focus as you read through James.

Chapter 1

A Lot of Controversy About a Little Book

What's Ahead

- James Who?
- Martin Luther's Beef
- Sermon on the Mount Redux

*C*hapters 2 through 13 of this study each examine a passage of verses from James. At first glance you might think that this chapter has no verses assigned to it. Not so fast. You've got reading to do for this chapter as well. In fact, we're suggesting you read the entire book of James at this initial stage. Don't worry—that's only a total of 108 verses. We'll give you a more specific reading assignment at the end of this chapter. But first, there are a few background details you should be aware of.

James Who?

We know that this epistle was written by James (1:1), but we don't know which one. *James* was apparently a pretty common Jewish name in the first century. So it is not surprising that several of those first Jewish Christians had this name. (There are six and possibly seven different people with this name mentioned in the New Testament.)

But since the author gave no specific details about himself other than his first name, scholars can do no better than narrow it down to four possible candidates (including two of the twelve disciples of Christ):

- *Candidate #1: James, the son of Zebedee.* James and his brother, John, were two of Christ's closest disciples. Peter, James, and John were in Christ's inner circle (see Mark 5:37; 9:2; 10:35; 14:33). This close personal friendship with Christ might make this James a possible choice for authorship, but most scholars believe he was martyred in AD 44, which is 20 years or so before the estimated date that the epistle of James was written (see Acts 12:2). As the pirates say, "Aaarh—dead men tell no tales," and they don't write epistles either. So, let's cross this James off the list.

- *Candidate #2: James, the son of Alphaeus.* This James was also one of the 12 disciples, but he blended into the background. As a disciple, he would have been known well enough to the relatively small community of Jewish Christians to just use his first name in the letter, but most scholars reject him as the actual author since he didn't appear to have a role of any prominence among the disciples. In other words, he is mentioned in the New Testament when the disciples are listed, but he never gets mentioned for doing anything. As you read through the book of James, you'll get the impression that the author was a doer, not a wallflower. So, let's vote James, the son Alphaeus off the list.

- *Candidate #3: James, the father of Judas.* There were two guys named Judas in the group of 12 disciples. The good one (not the one who betrayed Christ) is mentioned in Luke 6:16 and Acts 1:13 as "Judas, the son of James." Here again, we're dealing with someone named James who was known among the early Christians, but he doesn't appear to have sufficient "works" or "deeds" on his resume to make him a sure bet to be the author. If your only distinguishing feature is that you had a son named Judas, then you probably lack the gravitas to write a book like James. So, take this suspect off the list.

- *Candidate #4: James, the half-brother of Jesus.* In John 7:5, it is reported that Jesus had brothers who initially rejected Him as the Messiah; it turns out they didn't believe Him to be the Savior of the world until after the crucifixion and resurrection. (Let's face it. That entire resurrection thing can make a believer out of anyone, even a skeptical relative.) Actually, these were half-brothers of Jesus (they shared the same mother, but they were only half-brothers because Joseph was not the biological father of Jesus). After James changed his opinion about his half-brother's deity, he got involved in the burgeoning movement known as Christianity. So much so, that he eventually rose to a role of leadership in the Jerusalem church (the "mother" church for the Christian community).

We aren't advocating betting, but if there were going to be a wager on this issue, the smart money would be on James, the half-brother of Jesus, as the author of the epistle. As a leader in the church at Jerusalem, he would have the weight to speak with the authority that pervades this letter that is written to all of the "Jewish believers scattered abroad" (1:1).

A Word by *A*ny *O*ther *N*ame *M*eans the *S*ame

James is the name of the author, and it is also the name of the book we're studying. We don't want to get bogged down with extra verbiage by always distinguishing between "the author James" and the "the book of James." Most of the time we'll just refer to James, and hopefully the context will help you determine the correct reference we're making.

If you are new to Bible study, you might be confused by some other terminology. Obviously, the Bible is a book. But it is a compilation of 66 books, written by about 40 different authors over the span of roughly 1500 years. The Bible is divided into two major portions: The Old Testament (containing the first 39 books) and the New Testament (containing the last 27 books). Don't be confused; both testaments are old, so age has nothing to do with it. The division centers around Christ. The Old Testament books were written before His birth; the New Testament books were written after His death and resurrection. In the New Testament, the books are divided into these categories:

- Gospels (biographies of the life of Christ, named after their authors, Matthew, Mark, Luke, and John) at the beginning;

- a history book (Acts, telling the events of Christianity's spread through the Roman Empire during the decades immediately following the resurrection of Christ), which follows the Gospels;

- a book of prophecy (Revelation, the last book in the Bible); and

- epistles (actually letters written by guys like Paul, Peter, and John, to churches or individuals) sandwiched between Acts and Revelation.

James is one of the "books" of the Bible. But, because it is one of the New Testament books that was originally disseminated in letter form, we also refer to it as "the epistle of James."

Martin Luther's Beef

The great leader of the Protestant Reformation, Martin Luther, is famous for proclaiming the Gospel message that God's salvation is available to us through "grace alone." This concept—that salvation is a gift from God and there is nothing we can do to earn it—is clearly taught in Scripture, but it had apparently become obscured somewhere along the line in the first 1500 years of Christianity. Martin Luther put his life on the line to argue that salvation is not acquired by works or deeds on our part. Can you imagine then, how he felt when he read verses in the epistle of James like this one:

> *You see, faith by itself isn't enough. Unless it produces good deeds, it is dead and useless* (2:17).

Actually, you don't have to try to imagine his reaction. Here, from the first edition of his German New Testament (written in 1522) is his opinion of how the epistle of James stacks up against other New Testament books:

> Saint John's Gospel, and his first epistle, Saint Paul's epistles, especially those to the Romans, Galatians, Ephesians, and Saint Peter's first epistle—these are the books which show thee Christ, and teach thee everything that is needful and blessed for thee to know even though thou never see or hear any other book or doctrine. Therefore is Saint James's epistle a right strawy epistle in comparison with them, for it has no gospel character to it.

"No gospel character to it" seems to be a pretty good slam. And although we aren't experts in sixteenth-century lingo, "a right strawy epistle" seems like he is saying that James has the substance of straw and should be thrown into the Rhine River. (By the way, Martin Luther isn't alone in this assessment. Similar unflattering remarks have been repeated by many other commentators.)

Part of your challenge as you study the book of James will be to determine if Martin Luther was right, or wrong, or simply shortsighted. But as your guides on this journey, we don't want to leave you in suspense (plus, we want to sharpen your focus from the outset so you don't miss the rich teaching of James). So, we'll cut to the chase and explain that Martin Luther was so opposed to the Catholic Church's emphasis on "justification by works" that he missed the nuances in the epistle of James.

As you read and study through James, pay particular attention to how James clarifies the relationship between "faith" and "actions." Notice that he never says that good deeds are required to obtain salvation—rather, he seems to be giving us guidelines to determine whether our faith is genuine or fake. In that context, he says that good works are evidence of an authentic faith. In other words, actions don't give you salvation, but they are a good indicator of whether you are truly saved.

We'll get into this concept further in our study (particularly in James 2) but be on the lookout for this issue. It is a huge concept in James, and it can have life-transforming consequences for you.

$\mathcal{N}$umbers $\mathcal{C}$ount

When we give the citation for a verse, we'll use the standard format of giving the name of the book of the Bible, then the chapter and verse, separated by a colon. So, for example, Romans

12:1-2 refers to verses 1 and 2 in the twelfth chapter of the book of Romans.

But sometimes you'll see a chapter and verse citation that doesn't name the book, such as "The tongue is a small thing, but what enormous damage it can do" (3:5 TLB). This type of citation is to the chapter and verse in James. We aren't being lazy; we just figure that since this study is all about James, we can save several pages in each copy of this book (and thereby spare the lives of lots of trees) if we just drop the "James" reference instead of including it every time.

The Sermon on the Mount Redux

When you are reading through James, you might have a déjà vu moment back to when you last read the Sermon on the Mount, which Christ preached at the beginning of His public ministry. This famous passage of the New Testament (found in Matthew 5–7) contains Christ's teaching about the kingdom of God. While there is lots of theology jammed into that sermon, it packs a wallop due to its clarity and practical relevance. In other words, Jesus didn't talk about doctrinal intricacies—instead, He focused more on what the kingdom of God looks like in real life.

Watch for this same approach in James. Don't expect a doctrinal dissertation like you'll find in the first eleven chapters of Romans. Expect rather to find a Sermon-on-the-Mount approach that explains what authentic faith looks like in real life.

But there are more similarities than just that. James makes many direct references and allusions to the Sermon on the Mount. And for this reason, we're suggesting that you read the Sermon on the Mount (Matthew 5–7) in conjunction with a read-through of James. See if you can spot the thematic connections. To get you started, we'll give you a few (but there are lots more). Compare:

James	Sermon on the Mount
2:13	Matthew 6:14-15
4:11-12	Matthew 7:1-5
5:2-3	Matthew 6:19-21

Give It a Good Once-over

The book of James has been called the Proverbs of the New Testament. If you've read Proverbs, then you'll notice a structural similarity when you read through James. Proverbs has great, short, pithy sayings (which is why many people have a reading regimen of one verse or chapter from Proverbs each day). But it is difficult to spot themes and overarching topics in Proverbs because the verses or short passages often seem independent and disconnected with each other.

So it is with James. It has great verses with a lot of punch—they are very practical and don't get bogged down with a lot of doctrinal analysis. But sometimes it is difficult to see a continuing and cohesive theme in James. At first glance, a reader might think James was bouncing around from subject to subject, just following a random stream of consciousness. So, part of your challenge in this study will be to find the thematic underpinnings in the epistle. And there is no better time for doing that than your first time reading through the book.

■ ■ ■

$\mathcal{S}$tudy the $\mathcal{W}$ord

Read through James in its entirety. Make this reading for the purpose of getting an overall impression of the epistle as a whole. Then, answer these questions:

1. Try to imagine what it was like for James to grow up with Jesus as an older brother. Was life easier, or more difficult, for him? Why do you suppose James and his other brothers initially rejected the notion that Jesus was the long-awaited Messiah? Can you speculate on what might have changed his opinion? To gain some background on the position and prominence of James in the Jerusalem church, read Acts 12:17; 15:13-21; 21:18; and Galatians 2:9.

2. What is your overall impression of James after your initial reading of it? Does the book hold together thematically, or do you find it disjointed? What are the major themes you find?

3. Do you think James, as an author, speaks with authority? Do you think James was preaching *to* or *at* his audience? In other words, was this epistle intended to be an encouraging "pat on the back" or a corrective "kick in the rear"?

4. Did any verse or passage in particular jump out at you? Why? Is there a verse or passage that is confusing and demands more clarification? Did you read anything you don't agree with?

5. Can you summarize, in one or two sentences, the essential message of James?

If any of you wants to be my follower, you must put aside
your selfish ways, take up your cross, and follow me. If
you try to hang on to your life, you will lose it. But if you
give up your life for my sake, you will save it.

—*Jesus*

The Big Lie of the Christian Life

Doesn't it seem sometimes that Christians want to pretend life is great and doesn't involve any struggles? Personally, our experience is just the opposite. But as Christians, we are all guilty of trying to hide that fact. Okay, maybe we don't actually lie about it, but we certainly are slow to tell people that the Christian life often involves a lot of trials and tribulations (and that temptations aren't easily avoided either). Let's face it—we want Christianity to look good to other people. We don't want to focus on the tough aspects of it. So we put on a happy face and proceed to extol the positive aspects of the Christian life (while keeping our struggles). We justify this misrepresentation by rationalizing that, after all Christ has done for us, the least we can do is to fake it for Him.

But Christ never intended (and certainly never represented) that the Christian life was going to be a breeze. To the contrary, He used an analogy of picking up a cross—daily—if we were going to follow Him. Right there—that "cross" reference—is an indication that life as a Christian might be a little unpleasant at times.

Unlike many contemporary Christians, James comes out of the chute proclaiming that faith in Christ is going to have its share of tough times. But he says that is a good thing. Not because it is fun, but because tough times develop a mature faith.

Chapter 2

Is Your Faith Up to the Test?

James 1:1-12

What's Ahead

- From and To (1:1)
- So, You Got Trials? Congratulations! (1:2-4)
- Need Wisdom in How to Handle Tough Times? (1:5-11)
- Hang In There—The Best Is Yet to Come (1:12)

*U*nlike some of Paul's long salutations in his epistles where he elaborates on his affection for the group to whom he is writing, James is quick to get down to business. He has lots to say, and only 108 verses in which to get it said. So don't be surprised that he's blunt and to the point.

From and To (1:1)

As was the custom in the first century AD, James begins his letter with a salutation that reveals the identity of the author and the audience.

Notice how James refers to himself—as a slave of God and Jesus Christ. He isn't trying to play the "I'm important because I'm the half-brother of Jesus" card. We would be tempted to try to impress our readership with credentials (if we had any), but James isn't like that, because from his perspective, it is all about Jesus. So he doesn't try to raise his own status by referring to his blood relationship to Christ. Furthermore, when he does identify his relationship to Jesus, he says that it is as a slave to a master. He is likening his relationship to his brother to that of a slave, which in the culture of the first century was like being a piece of property that could be bought or sold at the will of the slave owner. This is James's not-so-subtle way of emphasizing the loyalty and obedience that a Christian owes to God (which will become relevant in a few verses when he discusses sticking with God's plan in the midst of difficulties).

The audience of this letter is the "Jewish Christians scattered among the nations." At the very beginning of Christianity, when Christ ascended to heaven after His resurrection, the prevailing view was that you had to first be a Jew to be a Christian. After all, Jesus was the Messiah of the Jews, who had been "God's chosen people" dating back about 1900 years in history, to the time of the patriarch Abraham. It wasn't until a few years after the resurrection that the early New Testament Christian church began to realize that God's plan of salvation was open to everyone—Jews and Gentiles alike.

By the time this letter was written, possibly between AD 44 and 49, the Jewish Christians had accepted (albeit reluctantly) the doctrine that Gentiles could become Christians by accepting Christ, without following all of the religious traditions that accompanied Judaism. But the Jewish Christians remained proud of their heritage, and that was part of the problem. So some leaders in the church, such as the apostle Paul, were telling the Jewish Christians they were hanging on to their traditions a little too tightly. In order to stop the Jewish Christians from imposing some of their traditions onto the Gentiles as a prerequisite for salvation, Paul (and others) hammered on the point that salvation had nothing to do with works:

> *God saved you by his grace when you believed. And you can't take credit for this; it is a gift from God. Salvation is not a reward for the good things we have done, so none of us can boast about it* (Ephesians 2:8-9).

This was a message the Jewish Christians needed to hear because they had a lot of cultural heritage. (The Gentiles, on the other hand, were more inclined to quickly grasp the concept that they had nothing to bring to God's salvation table.) But maybe the Jewish Christians were taking Paul's message to an unhealthy extreme. Maybe James felt compelled to make sure they realized that, while works had nothing to do with salvation, actions still remained a valid indicator of the legitimacy of a person's faith.

So, You Got Trials? Congratulations! (1:2-4)

It sounds strange, and perhaps a bit harsh, but James wanted his readers to be joyful in the midst of their suffering. This is such a counterintuitive notion that it requires some explanation:

- *Suffering:* Christians in the first century knew quite a bit about suffering. It was much more than some pagan calling them a "goody two-shoes" or a "Bible thumper." (Actually, they were *never* called a "Bible thumper" because the Bible hadn't been compiled yet.) Rather they were living under the prospect of being thrown into a lion-filled arena because of their faith. Persecution and poverty were rampant in the early church. Times were perilous for these new believers. Any association with Christianity could mean that a Jew would be ostracized by the Jewish community, which was opposed to the upstart followers of Christ. From the Jewish hierarchy, a new Christian might face social and economic ruin. From the Roman authorities, a Christian might face death. (This puts your problems into perspective a bit, doesn't it?)

- *Joy:* James doesn't say that his hearers should be happy in the middle of tough times. He doesn't expect them to be giddy in the face of dangerous and oppressive circumstances. But he does want them to realize they can find joy in the situation. From a spiritual perspective, 1) joy includes aspects of peace and tranquility because we know that God is ultimately in control; 2) it encompasses attitudes of appreciation and thankfulness for God's concern for us; and 3) it entails assurance and expectation of an eventual outcome according to God's plan.

Jesus knew this kind of joy in the midst of extreme suffering:

> He was willing to die a shameful death on the cross because of the joy he knew would be his afterwards (Hebrews 12:2 TLB).

And other New Testament writers, such as Paul, often wrote about this same principle:

> I will rejoice even if I lose my life, pouring it out like a liquid offering to God, just like your faithful service is an offering to God. And I want all of you to share that joy...For God's way of making

*us right with himself depends on faith. I want
to know Christ and experience the mighty power
that raised him from the dead. I want to suffer
with him, sharing in his death, so that one way
or another I will experience the resurrection from
the dead!* (Philippians 2:17-18; 3:9-11).

Much like an infant grows over time to adulthood, a
person's faith has a growth progression. In its infancy, a
person's faith may be weak (and a little immature). But,
importantly, it shouldn't stay this way. Faith should
mature to the point where it is strong and solid. James
emphasizes that growth process by saying that we build
up spiritual endurance as we go through tough times. As
our endurance grows, so does our spiritual character. That's
what being a Christian is all about—our character keeps
growing, changing, and developing as we become more
Christlike:

*The Lord—who is the Spirit—makes us more and
more like him as we are changed into his glorious
image* (2 Corinthians 3:18).

Need Wisdom in How to Handle
Tough Times? (1:5-11)

James is being a little rhetorical in verse 5 when he asks
if any of us needs wisdom to get through tough times. The
expected answer is a resounding "Yes!" When the going
gets rough, most of us are at a loss for what to do, in both
the spiritual realm and in the practicalities of everyday life.
On the spiritual and theological level, we want to know,
*Why does God allow these things? Does He still love us? What
do we do when our faith is getting shaky?* On the practical
level, we need wisdom for issues such as, *How do we repair*

a broken relationship? Where is the money going to come from to pay the bills? How can we get healthy and stop the pain?

Pray About It

James isn't telling us anything new when he suggests, almost offhandedly, that all we need to do is ask God for wisdom and He'll give it to us. Most of us are quick to pray and ask for wisdom when we are up against the wall. But James does give us some clues about why our prayers might not be as effective as we would like.

Have a Confident Expectation

Our prayers for wisdom and guidance in tough times should be wrapped in an expectation that God will answer our request with the wisdom we need. He doesn't want us waffling back and forth (like waves in the ocean) in our attitude about prayer, or in our commitment to follow His wisdom when He gives it to us. When we pray, we need to be convinced He will make good on His promise to deliver wisdom to us. And we need to be equally committed to respond to His revealed wisdom and follow His directions. Wavering back and forth about either His commitment, or ours, will undercut the effectiveness of our prayers.

Have the Right Spirit

Verses 9 through 11 might be one of those spots where you think James is going off on a tangent. Not really, but you have to read these verses in the context of what preceded them: The attitude we should have when we are praying for wisdom.

In addition to having a confident expectancy that God will answer and we will obey, James wants us to pray with the right attitude about our relationship to God. For those who are poor, he wants them to realize that their momentary poverty on earth is nothing compared to the spiritual riches they will enjoy for all eternity as a child of God. And for those who happen to be wealthy on earth, James wants them to pray in humility, recognizing that earthly riches can fade faster than a delicate flower in the scorching sun.

Maybe God Is Offering Wisdom, but You Aren't Seeing It

When you pray for God's wisdom, how are you expecting He is going to answer your prayer and deliver the wisdom you need? Let's admit that, for the most part, His days of sending a host of messenger angels is over. Nor does He implement anymore that big booming voice from the sky. And the handwriting on the wall hasn't appeared in centuries. So how are you going to get your divine wisdom?

God often conveys wisdom to us through one of three ways (or a combination of them, depending upon how dense we are):

- *Wisdom from His Word:* The Bible is a rich source of God's wisdom. Maybe the answer to your prayer is in there. But that means you've got to be reading it. Don't worry about finding just the right passage. Don't feel compelled to close your eyes and randomly point to a verse, hoping you've hit the right one. Just start reading. God will honor your search. "Your word is a lamp to my feet and a light for my path...The unfolding of your words gives light; it gives understanding to the simple" (Psalm 119:105,130).

- *Wisdom from the Holy Spirit:* Sometimes we forget that as Christians, we have God's Holy Spirit living within us. Sometimes we need to sit still long enough to hear what He is saying to us. "I will put my law in their minds and write it on their hearts" (Jeremiah 31:33 NIV).

> • *Wisdom from other Christians:* Remember that God uses other Christians as His hands, and feet, and mouth. If He wants to speak to you, isn't it reasonable that He might use other Christians to tell you the wisdom He wants you to hear? "With good counselors there is safety" (Proverbs 11:14 TLB).

Hang In There—the Best Is Yet to Come (1:12)

James brings this discussion full circle in verse 12, by returning to the issue of endurance during tough times. Persevering under trials is a sign of spiritual maturity. The difficulties, no matter how great, do not distract a Christian of mature faith from seeing the big picture.

When James talks about receiving a reward of a "crown of life," he is not referring to an actual crown. He is using an athletic metaphor that would have been recognized by his readers. In the Greek and Roman athletic competitions (think early Olympics), a wreath was placed on the head of the victorious competitor. This crown did not have value in and of itself, but it was valuable for what it represented.

Paul often used this same type of metaphor to convey the same thought:

> *I have fought the good fight, I have finished the race, and I have remained faithful. And now the prize awaits me—the crown of righteousness, which the Lord, the righteous Judge, will give me on the day of his return. And the prize is not just for me but for all who eagerly look forward to his appearing* (2 Timothy 4:7-8).

In the Christian life, we don't walk around wearing crowns on our heads (except at a kid's birthday party at Burger King). But we know we already have the invaluable reward of a spiritual relationship with God—and after our troubles have ended when our earthly existence is over, then we will be enjoying the prize of eternal life in the presence of our heavenly Father.

Without intending to minimize our earthly troubles, James wants us to realize that a few years of misery on earth pales in comparison to an eternity in heaven. That understanding should be a motivation that helps us endure the tough times.

■ ■ ■

Study the Word

1. Why do many religious people like to have rules to follow? In the context of the early stages of Christianity, how could the Jewish traditions be helpful? In what situations could they be harmful?

2. When difficult times come into your life, what is your immediate reaction? Is it positive or something else? When this has happened in the past, how have you approached God about it?

3. What is James's perspective on suffering in a Christian's life?

4. Based on what you have already learned from chapter 1 of James, what counsel could you give to a Christian friend who is in the middle of a big problem?

5. Has there been a time in your life when you patiently endured and sought God through a difficulty and later realized that your faith had become stronger through the process?

It is incredible how easily human beings blame the
gods and believe us to be the source of the troubles,
when it is their own wickedness and stupidity that
brings upon them sorrows more severe than any
which Destiny would assign.

—*Zeus (from Homer's* Odyssey)

*A*re *Y*ou *T*rying to *G*ive *G*od the *B*lame?

The natural human instinct is to blame someone else for our problems. If you doubt it, then just think about how two little kids in a family will respond when confronted by their mother and father, who are upset over a broken lamp in the living room. Those guilty kids, with the soccer ball still rolling around their feet, will be quick to blame anyone or anything else: *The cat did it. The wind did it. Mikey from next door came over to play and did it.* (Parents are sharp. They see right through these lies. Especially since they don't own a cat, there is no wind inside the house, and the neighbor family is on vacation.) So, when blame can't be attached elsewhere, then rationalizations come into play: *My brother made me do it.*

Christians take the same approach to sin. We know it is wrong, so when we do it, we like to shift the blame elsewhere. Satan is an easy target. And if we can't pin it on him, then we try to get theologically creative and blame God through a multistep rationalization. (If you haven't gotten this sophisticated in your blame-shifting, then don't get started with it.)

In the passage we're studying in this chapter, James confronts the issue of blame-shifting. Here's the bottom line: Are you trying to reclassify the problems created by your sin into "trials" brought into your life by God? Get ready. It's gut-check time.

Chapter 3

Are You Falling for Your Own Temptation?

James 1:13-18

What's Ahead

- It's Not God's Fault (1:13)
- The Progression from Temptation to Death (1:14-16)
- God Is a Good Gift Giver (1:16-18)

*B*efore we proceed, let's review. In the last passage we studied (which was also the first passage we studied), James talked about the benefit of standing firm in our faith while we endure tough times. Not only is our faith strengthened and matured in this process, but also the experience involves the spiritual reward of God's presence. In this context, tough times are a good thing because God is using them in our lives for His purposes to strengthen our faith in Him. Isn't that what Christianity is all about?

Does this mean that God has brought all of life's problems to us so He can achieve His purposes for us? Absolutely not. Many of the difficult circumstances in our lives are simply the consequences of our sin. Whether our sin takes the form of bad choices or improper conduct, the results often turn out to be a messed-up life. Is that God's fault? No, it's our own fault. But it seems a lot easier to live with ourselves (and other Christians) if we can recharacterize the whole scenario as trouble that God brought our way instead of admitting to ourselves (and other Christians) that we are suffering from the effects of our sin.

In the passage before us, James deals with the tendency to rationalize the disastrous consequences of sin as being God's fault (or at least His responsibility). In his usual blunt manner, James puts the blame for sin squarely where it belongs.

It's Not God's Fault (1:13)

There is a "God made me sin" rationalization that goes something like this:

- God is sovereign (meaning He has supreme authority and power over every single thing that happens in the universe).

- I sinned when I was tempted by certain circumstances (I got blind drunk when I went to that party; I cheated on my taxes because the tax bill was too high; I yell at my spouse and kids because they never give me "alone time"; and so on).

- Since God controls the circumstances of the universe, He allowed those circumstances into my life.

- Thus, since I was tempted by those circumstances, God was the one who tempted me.

Another rationalization—"these problems are God's fault"—is closely related in its logical deficiencies:

- I admit it; I have problems in my life that are the result of my own sin.

- God is allowing me to stew in the juices of these problems.

- But God is sovereign and controls the circumstances of the universe.

- God has the power to get me out of this predicament, but He is refusing to do so.

- Since God could stop these problems but isn't doing so, then these problems are really God's fault.

Whether the rationalization is over the *cause* (giving in to temptation) or the *result* (the consequences of our sin), James candidly sets our thinking straight. We can't blame God, because He had nothing to do with the initial temptation.

There Is a Difference Between Trials and Temptations

It doesn't appear as noticeably in our English translations of the Bible, but verse 13 begins a shift of terminology that is more readily apparent in the original Greek language used by James. The words like *testing, trials,* and *trouble* in 1:2 (which are an opportunity for our joy) are distinguished from *temptation,* which is addressed by James in the present passage. Although all of these words reflect the same Greek word group, they have disparate meanings when used in the Bible. *Testing, trials,* and *troubles* are from God and are used by Him for our spiritual development; *temptation,* on the other hand, is the precursor to sin and is something we get into ourselves.

- *Sometimes God tests us as a group of believers.* He did this with Israelites when Moses led them in the desert. "Remember how the LORD your God led you through the wilderness for these forty years, humbling you and testing you to prove your character, and to find out whether or not you would obey his commands" (Deuteronomy 8:2).

- *Sometimes God tests us individually.* God tested Abraham's faith when He instructed Abraham to sacrifice his son Isaac: "Abraham!...Take your son...and go to the land of Moriah. Go and sacrifice him as a burnt offering on one of the mountains, which I will show you" (Genesis 22:1-2). Just in case you don't know the end of the story, Abraham proved his faith by proceeding as God had instructed, but God stopped Abraham at the last minute after Abraham's faith was displayed.

- *Sometimes God allows us to go through a trial.* That's what happened when God allowed Satan to wreak havoc in Job's life through the deaths of his children, economic ruin, and medical ailments. Job would agree with James that there is a strengthening of your faith when you endure with God through difficult trials: "I have stayed on God's paths; I have followed his ways and not turned aside. I have not departed from his commands, but have treasured his words more than daily food. But once he has made his decision, who can change his mind? Whatever he wants to do, he does. So he will do for me whatever he has planned. He controls my destiny" (Job 23:11-14).

But tests and trials have nothing to do with sin. Sin is conceived in the womb of temptation, and God has nothing to do with that.

God Doesn't Play the Temptation Game

To reinforce the distinction, James states it succinctly in verse 13:

- *God is never tempted to do wrong.* It is contrary to His character. God and evil are mutually exclusive. Since

God and evil cannot co-exist, God is immune to the temptation to sin. "He [Jesus Christ] is the kind of high priest we need because he is holy and blameless, unstained by sin" (Hebrews 7:26).

- *God never tempts anyone else either.* Since He abhors sin, God is not going to entice or tempt anyone to commit it. When Jesus Christ was led out into the wilderness to be tempted by Satan, God was not a conspirator in the temptation. Satan's intent was all about temptation, but from God's perspective the episode was all about revealing the endurance of Christ's faith (and He did persevere). You can find the entire narrative in Matthew 4:1-11.

Temptation is a favorite ploy of Satan, not God. But Satan isn't solely to blame when we stumble into sin. Sometimes Satan isn't even remotely involved. We have the knack of putting ourselves into places and situations where we're tempted to sin without any involvement on Satan's part.

God gets blamed for a lot of problems that He didn't bring into our lives.

Satan gets blamed for a lot of problems that we initiated on our own.

The Progression from Temptation to Death (1:14-16)

James proceeds to clarify that temptation comes from sources other than God. He explains that temptation is initiated within our own evil desires. Even if temptation is put in our path by Satan, he can't make us sin. It is our own lust or greed or vanity that we allow to overtake us. It all starts within ourselves:

> *The human heart is most deceitful of all things.*
> *Who really knows how bad it is?* (Jeremiah
> 17:9).

Sometimes there is a sin trap that we fall into unsuspectingly (which usually means that we are in a place we don't belong). We don't plan on sinning, but we just end up doing it without thinking. Other times, we might be more intentional with our sin business. With full knowledge, we allow ourselves to be lured into temptation by an appeal we don't want to resist.

Once we give rein to our improper desires, then they morph into evil actions or conduct that is inappropriate. The consequences of such action are fatal.

The death that comes from our sin isn't necessarily physical death (although it could get that bad). When James uses the *death* term, he is speaking in a more metaphysical sense. Our sin can kill friendships, marriages, our happiness, trust, financial security, and the list goes on. Most importantly, our unconfessed sin momentarily kills our fellowship with God.

James Wants to Make This Point Unmistakable

Verse 16—which says, "Don't be misled"—is another one of the "pop up" verses that James sticks in from time to time. He's basically saying, "Hey, guys—don't miss this point." Apparently, James wasn't as specific as he should have been because there is debate about which point he's referring to.

Some scholars believe the point James is trying to emphasize is from the prior verse (1:15—improper thoughts produce improper actions that result in death). Other scholars believe James is trying to flag the importance of the following verse (1:17—that only good things come from God).

We aren't so sure that is it only one point or the other. We think James made that statement when he was caught up in the excitement of declaring the entire concept that we're responsible for our own sin and shouldn't try to pin it on God.

God Is a Good Gift Giver (1:16-18)

Earlier, in verse 13, James told us what God's character is *not:* It is not capable of sinning and not capable of tempting others to sin. In verses 17-18, James gives us a brief glimpse into what God's character *is:* It is everything good. James says that if something is good, then it comes from God. Whether it is health, the weather, friendships, or truth, God is responsible for the good things you enjoy in life.

But the goodness of God is apparent not only in the things He provides. There are also beneficial aspects of His character, such as His unchanging nature. This is a common theme that runs throughout Scripture:

> *I am the LORD, and I do not change* (Malachi 3:6).

> *Jesus Christ is the same yesterday, today, and forever* (Hebrews 13:8).

The loving nature of God, and His forgiveness and grace, wouldn't mean very much if He had a mercurial temperament and constantly and unpredictably changed His moods. But He is not that way at all. He is steady and unchangeable. That is why we can depend upon Him as we endure the hardships of life.

James concludes this dissertation on resisting the urge to blame God for the consequences of our sin by reminding us of the best evidence of God's goodness: our salvation. The efforts God made to save us from the eternal consequences of our sin were not inconsequential. His Son paid the penalty for our sin on the cross so we might be called His children:

> *See how very much our Father loves us, for he calls us his children, and that is what we are!* (1 John 3:1).

And God has provided us with the His Word, which reveals the grand design of His eternal plan for us:

> *How we praise God, the Father of the Lord Jesus Christ, who has blessed us with every spiritual blessing in heaven because we belong to Christ... And...all you others too...heard the Good News about how to be saved* (Ephesians 1:3,13 TLB).

As His children, we are not just one of His creations. We are His most prized possession. With goodness like that, we can understand that God has no role in the circumstances of our temptation. Looks like we have no one else to blame for the consequences of our sin except ourselves.

■ ■ ■

*S*tudy the *W*ord

1. What are the excuses people use to rationalize away their sin?

2. Why are we reluctant to accept responsibility for the consequences of our own sin?

3. Do you agree that God shouldn't be blamed for the circumstances of our temptation even though He has the ability to change those circumstances before they happen? Does the fact He is sovereign make Him responsible in some way?

4. What is the progression of sin, from inception to final result, as explained by James?

5. What would happen to the doctrines of Christianity if God's character were not unchangeable?

We might wonder why the ever-practical James does not proceed to outline schemes of daily Bible reading or the like, for surely these are the ways in which we offer a willing ear to the voice of God. But he does not help us in this way. Rather, he goes deeper for there is little point in schemes and times if we have not got an attentive spirit.

—J.A. Motyer

Don't Fake It

According to 1 Samuel 16:7, "People judge by outward appearance, but the LORD looks at the heart."

If people look only at the outward trappings, then faking a genuine Christian life is pretty easy. All that is required is to dress and act the part: go to church, carry a Bible, give some money, handle some volunteer projects, and quote a Bible verse from time to time. Whether you love God or not doesn't matter, because people can't see what is really in your heart.

But God doesn't limit His assessment to the shallow standards used by people. He looks deep inside to see if your faith is genuine. You can't pull a fast one on God because He knows what you are really thinking.

The passage we're studying in this chapter reveals that James has concerns about people who are merely playing at Christianity. He wants their faith to be authentic, so he challenges them to put the principles of God's Word into action. If you have trouble moving biblical principles from the page into the reality of your life, you might be helped by the steps James suggests.

Chapter 4

Does the Word Affect
More than Just Your Ears?

James 1:19-27

What's Ahead

- Have the Right Mind-set for God's Word (1:19-20)
- Moral Purity and Humility (1:21)
- Don't Just Look, Do Something (1:22-25)
- Let Me Give You Two Examples (1:26-27)

James 1:19-27 begins a new thought. We don't want to be critical, so excuse us if we say that James did a less-than-stellar job making a smooth transition from the previous thought into this one. But hey, if we applaud his brevity and down-to-business approach in some passages, perhaps we shouldn't complain if he doesn't waste a lot of words making transitions.

As our last passage concluded (1:18), James was reminding us that God's goodness was evidenced by His giving us His Word, which helped bring us to salvation. Now, beginning with verse 19, James is going to talk about making sure we live in a way that reflects what God's Word teaches. In other words, he wants us to "walk the talk." So, to get you in the right frame of mind, read verse 18, and right before reading verse 19, pretend that James said something like, "Speaking

45

of God's Word, let me say a few things about living in conformity with its principles."

Have the Right Mind-set for God's Word (1:19-20)

Remember that James was writing to Jewish Christians spread out among fledgling churches throughout the Roman Empire. While those Christians were diverse in their geographical locations, they apparently had a few undesirable traits in common. As we'll see now and later in our study of James, these Christians needed correction, and James was using his letter to give it to them. He wants to put them back on track, spiritually speaking, and to do so, he needs to get them reflecting on God's Word.

This is a good principle for all of us to remember. Without constantly comparing ourselves to the biblical principles of our faith, we're likely to deviate from them. Following Christ's teaching is an essential component of being one of His disciples:

> Jesus said to the people who believed in him, "You are truly my disciples if you remain faithful to my teachings" (John 8:31).

Oftentimes we can't hear God speaking to us because we are too busy spouting off with our own opinions and complaints. James knew this was a common malady. His solution to correct the problem begins with a simple step: He tells his readers to shut up. But he says it with a little more Christian style, and he lays it out in a logical sequence:

- *Be quick to listen:* If we are to hear from God, directly or through others, we've got to stop talking and griping, and we must be quiet enough, for long enough, so we can hear what God is trying to say to us. This instruction is one of the reasons why people see similarities between James and Proverbs: "Even fools are thought wise when they keep silent; with their mouths shut, they seem intelligent" (Proverbs 17:28).

- *Be slow to speak:* Often, our initial reaction isn't our best one. Our visceral response is often not a Christ-like reply. We can do much better if we withhold our comments until we give the Holy Spirit time to influence our reactions. Here again, James's instruction is aligned with the wisdom of Proverbs: "There is more hope for a fool than for someone who speaks without thinking" (Proverbs 29:20).

- *Be slow to get angry:* Despite being the target of abusive treatment, Christ was hardly ever angry. On the rare occasion when it happened—such as when He drove the money changers from the temple (Matthew 21:12-13)—it was a reaction to people's disrespect for God's holiness. Christ never responded in anger to His own mistreatment. Anger is simply not an effective technique for dealing with problems. If we are angry, we can't objectively process comments from other people. More importantly, our anger can close our ears to what God is trying to say to us. Proverbs 19:19 explains it this way: "Hot-tempered people must pay the penalty."

With the Jewish heritage of his readers, the parallels in these statements by James to the wisdom literature of Proverbs were readily recognizable to them. What he is saying, between the lines, is that they need to quiet things down—their own volume and their own blood pressure—to assume a proper mind-set for letting God's Word penetrate their hearts.

Moral Purity and Humility (1:21)

Quietness of spirit is a good spiritual discipline that positions us to hear from God.

> *Be still, and know that I am God!* (Psalm 46:10).

James suggested this as a first step, but it isn't the only step that is required to prepare for the application of God's Word to our lives. James also believes we must approach God's Word with moral purity and humility.

Moral Purity

The world is full of junk, and we often fill our hearts and minds with it. So much so, that there is no room left over for God. If we are serious about conforming our lives to what the Bible teaches, we need to make room in our lives for God. That means clearing out the clutter.

James isn't talking about mere distractions (a busy schedule, an in-box stacked high with papers, unanswered e-mails, or unfinished projects). He is talking about matters in our lives that constitute sin by their very nature. He wants us to get rid of the filth and evil in our lives. His references indicate that we are to address moral impurity by intentional action.

Peter also taught this same principle. In his first epistle, he emphasized the importance of the Word of God in bringing salvation to us:

> *You have been born again, but not to a life that will quickly end. Your new life will last forever because it comes from the eternal, living word of God...And that word is the Good News that was preached to you* (1 Peter 1:23-25).

And after laying down this principle, he immediately

stresses the importance of moral purity as we seek to acquire more spiritual sustenance:

> *So get rid of all evil behavior. Be done with all*
> *deceit, hypocrisy, jealousy, and all unkind speech.*
> *Like newborn babies, you must crave pure spiritual*
> *milk so that you will grow into a full experience*
> *of salvation. Cry out for this nourishment, now*
> *that you have had a taste of the Lord's kindness*
> (1 Peter 2:1-3).

What are we left with if we get rid of all of our foul thoughts? Does God want us to be empty-headed? Absolutely not. He wants our minds filled with thoughts that drive us closer to Him:

> *Fix your thoughts on what is true, and honorable,*
> *and right, and pure, and lovely, and admirable.*
> *Think about things that are excellent and worthy*
> *of praise* (Philippians 4:8).

Our best chance at drawing maximum understanding from God Word occurs when we begin with a mind that is on His wave length.

Humility

James also wanted his readers to approach God's Word with the right attitude. Correct thinking (thoughts that are good, right, and true), must be accompanied by a proper perspective. We need to internalize our unworthiness to receive God's saving grace.

Some Christians approach God like they are doing Him a favor. They are proud and arrogant though they have no justification for it. Such attitudes are obstacles to receiving spiritual truth from the study of God's Word. Instead, James suggests we approach God with a teachable and submissive spirit.

Why should we approach the study of the gospel message with such reverence and humbleness? Because it was the hearing of the Gospel that led to our salvation in the first place (see Ephesians 1:13). This message is not forced upon us by God. He isn't cramming it down our throats. He offers it to us. And James describes it as a message we "accept" like a gift that is presented to us.

Don't Just Look, Do Something (1:22-25)

James has set the stage. He has said we need to approach God with a quiet and receptive spirit, having gotten rid of the intentional sinful rebellion in our lives and being reverent, humble, and teachable. Equally important, however, is our response *after* we have encountered God's message.

Hearing and receiving God's instruction is one thing. Applying it is another matter.

James uses the analogy of a mirror to emphasize the absurdity of listening to God's Word without applying it. Understanding the nature of human vanity, James suggests that none of us would look at ourselves in the mirror without correcting a fashion faux pas. He's right, isn't he? Suppose you make one last double-check of your appearance before joining a group of friends. Everything in the mirror looks fine until you smile. Then you notice, stuck between your front teeth, a bit of that spinach salad you had for lunch. Unfortunately, it isn't a fragment from the hard-boiled egg white. Nope, as luck would have it, it is part of a spinach leaf, in a shade of green so bright that it's almost luminous.

Now, would any of us simply walk away without removing the offending vegetable fragment? Of course not. Even if it means trying to floss with a shoelace or using a car key as a toothpick, we're going to plant ourselves in front of that mirror until we have removed that green morsel and restored our smile to its pristine condition, sans veggie distractions. Simply put, we're going to change ourselves based on the flaws the mirror reveals.

We should approach God's Word with the same concern for self-improvement. Even though we try to approach God in the right spirit and with the right attitude, we're far from perfect. Examining our lives in the reflection of God's Word will reveal quite a few vegetable bits in our teeth (spiritually speaking). Is it appropriate for us to walk away without making any adjustments—and later forget entirely about the flaws we saw? To the contrary, we should immediately commit to the Lord that we want to correct the problems in our lives that His Word reveals.

Repentance Is a Change of Behavior

There is a form of repentance that is integral to salvation: an acknowledgment and confession that our sin can be forgiven only by Christ's death on the cross. "We are made right with God by placing our faith in Jesus Christ" (Romans 3:22). And while God's forgiveness is sufficient to cover our sins—past, present, and future—ongoing confession is important because it removes the obstacles to ongoing fellowship with God.

Repentance is more than saying "I'm sorry" to God. It involves the intent to refrain from further sin in the future. The word picture associated with *repentance* is a person who is walking one way, and then turns around, making a diametric change in his or her direction.

If we are truly repentant for our sins, then we will make changes in our lifestyle to avoid repeating them.

If someone claims, "I know God," but doesn't obey God's commandments, that person is a liar and is not living in the truth. But those who obey God's word truly show how completely they love him. That is how we know we are living in him. Those who say they live in God should live their lives as Jesus did (1 John 2:4-6).

Let Me Give You Two Examples (1:26-27)

James proceeds to give two examples of what it looks like if someone is a "hearer only" but not a "doer" of God's Word. One of his examples is negative (things we know we shouldn't do), and the other one is positive (things we know we should do):

- *Uncontrolled speech:* The Bible is replete with cautions for us to avoid malicious speech, including gossip and lies. If we aren't intentional about guarding what we say, then James suggests our faith may be a sham.

- *Aiding the defenseless:* Two of the weakest segments of first-century society were widows and orphans. James says if our faith is genuine, then we will care for people who do not have the ability to care for themselves. This is counterintuitive. It doesn't come naturally to us. And it is countercultural. It isn't a popular thing to be doing. But we must resist our natural tendencies and go against society's trends if we are to follow God's pattern.

Looking into the mirror of God's Word will reveal the things we should do and the things we shouldn't be doing. Whether or not we follow through is an indicator of whether we sincerely believe what we claim to be our faith. If we don't, then we are only fooling ourselves, because we certainly aren't fooling God.

■ ■ ■

$\mathcal{S}$tudy the $\mathcal{W}$ord

1. At the beginning and end of this passage (1:19 and 1:26), James talks about controlling your speech. Why do you think he places so much emphasis on controlling the tongue?

2. If all of our sins (past, present, and future) are forgiven at the moment of our salvation, why does our sinful behavior, if unconfessed, interfere with our fellowship with God?

3. Can you think of another analogy, besides a mirror, which can illustrate the foolishness of being made aware of a flaw but declining to do something about it? Apply this new analogy to the lesson you have learned from James about the spiritual life.

4. What are some examples of hypocrisy in people who claim to be Christians but who do not exhibit Christ-like behavior? Are there instances in your life that reveal inconsistency between the faith you claim and the faith you exhibit?

5. James identified the widows and orphans as the helpless people in his society. Who are the groups in your community who are helpless? Why might we be reluctant to make helping the defenseless an important focus of our faith?

Consider, at the outset,
how great a majority are the poor.

—*Seneca*
(Roman statesman and philosopher,
4 BC–AD 65)

Assessing Whether You've Got It or Not

Humility can be deceptive. The moment you become proud because you think you have attained it, then by its very definition, you've lost it.

Favoritism and prejudice are equally deceptive. Some people, who believe they aren't prejudiced, might be unknowingly exhibiting favoritism to a certain group. To treat one group with favoritism is, implicitly, to be prejudiced against others who aren't part of the favored group.

In the passage in this chapter, we'll be looking at intentional favoritism (and, conversely, unintended discrimination). Interestingly, James uses behavior in the church to illustrate this problem.

This passage will give us a good opportunity to examine our own motives and actions. Maybe we'll find we're guilty of doing something that we weren't even aware of.

Chapter 5

Are You Taking Part in Partiality?

James 2:1-13

*J*ames 2 marks the beginning of a new thought (but not really). James begins a 13-verse discussion about the dangers of showing favoritism in the church; this is a new thought. But he left off (in 1:27) by declaring that true faith in Christ involves helping the defenseless widows and orphans. Thus there is a connection to the former passage, because the favoritism he decries was being shown to the rich, meaning that the poor (such as widows and orphans) were being discriminated against, because they didn't receive preferred treatment.

Throughout the Roman Empire in the first century, there was essentially no middle class. Either you were privileged or you lived in poverty. Historians believe that approximately 8 to 10 percent of the population had wealth; the remaining 90 percent or so were poor. And there was almost no opportunity to climb up the socioeconomic ladder. So if you were poor, you stayed poor.

The wealthy, privileged class was well entrenched in its status. They had all of the power (or at least had access to it), so they were able to ensure their continued standing. Their advantages included authority and economic leverage over the lower class. They were in an enviable position. And those in the lower class did just that—envied the possessions and social control enjoyed by the rich.

The wealthy were notorious for abusing their power and authority over the poor. Consequently, the poor were compelled to act in a subservient and obsequious manner toward the rich, simply as a matter of self-preservation. But they also did so in an effort to cater to and win the favor of the members of the upper class. They acted nicer toward the rich (because of what they might get from them) than they acted toward other members of their own poverty class.

While showing such favoritism is understandable, it is contrary to biblical teaching. James is going to point that out. He knows that this will be a difficult message for his readers to hear, so he softens the blow by beginning with "my dear brothers and sisters" (2:1). He wants to make sure they are convinced of his love for them before he punches them between the eyes.

Do You Want to Know How God Feels About the Poor?

This message came to Zechariah from the LORD: "This is what the LORD of Heaven's Armies says: Judge fairly, and show mercy and kindness to one another. Do not oppress widows, orphans, foreigners, and the poor" (Zechariah 7:9-10).

Get the Fashion Police out of Your Church (2:1-4)

James begins with a rhetorical question: How can you claim to be a Christian if you show kindness to some people more than others? He is not asking the question because he is searching for an answer. He knows the answer, and so do his readers. The answer was obvious to everyone—Christ never showed favoritism, and neither should His followers.

As the discussion will reveal, James was not talking about being nice to someone. Christ would certainly endorse that approach. Instead, the subject of James's criticism is being unduly nice to one person while being far less kind to someone else. James characterizes such treatment as showing *favoritism* to the preferred group, and *discriminating* against the other group.

James starts getting personal when he brings the discussion into his readers' own churches. He asks them to envision a situation that was, without a doubt, a real-life scenario for most of them. Two people enter the church. They are both "first-time attenders" because they do not know where to sit. One of them is dressed in expensive clothes and has all of the appropriate accessories; the other is dressed in clothes that were purchased at the local the thrift shop (from the "Any Item—25 Cents" barrel). The obviously wealthy person is escorted to a comfortable seat with a preferred view. The observably poor visitor, however, is told to stand at the back of the room, behind a pillar if possible.

James is not upset that the rich person is shown kindness and courtesy. Rather, he is outraged that the poor person does not receive similar treatment. He implies that every person, regardless of economic status, should be showed such kindness. The fact that his readers weren't extending equal treatment proved they had the wrong motives when they favored the rich and discriminated against the poor.

You Shouldn't Get Caught Up in the World's Perspective (2:5-7)

While the poor may be irrelevant from the culture's viewpoint, James is quick to point out to his readers that the poor are not overlooked by God. Although they may be poor by earthly standards, they can be rich by spiritual standards. Regardless of our bank-account balances, we as Christians have every spiritual blessing available to us (Ephesians 1:3). God's riches extend to all who believe in Him (Romans 10:12). Earthly economics is immaterial because we have heavenly riches and spiritual blessings:

> Our hearts ache, but we always have joy. We are poor, but we give spiritual riches to others. We own nothing, and yet we have everything (2 Corinthians 6:10).

Since God places such a high value on His children, regardless of their material possessions, then it is an insult for the rest of us to disregard any of them so quickly.

James goes further and points out the irony of extending privileged treatment to the wealthy. It was the rich of the society who instituted civil lawsuits against the poor. Often the end result was to taint the name of Christ and of Christianity:

- Sometimes, Christians were prosecuted for their faith;
- other times, Christians were sued for debts owed to the wealthy; and
- occasionally, a wealthy person claiming to be a Christian would sue a less fortunate Christian.

Whenever one of these things happened, the name of Christ was sullied. Why should Christians extend favoritism to those who discredited the name of Christ? James wants us to think through the logical consequences of our favoritism and discrimination.

Because the Bible Says So (2:8-12)

To hammer home his point, James now brings out the big gun—a specific reference to the Law. Nothing was more sacred to a Jew.

Love Your Neighbor (Even the Poor Ones)

The passage quoted by James was so well-known to these Jewish Christians, it was not necessary for him to remind them that Moses had transcribed the words as part of God's commandments recorded in the book of Leviticus:

> Love your neighbor as yourself (Leviticus 19:18).

But it wasn't only an ancient command of God uttered centuries before. They would have also known that, more recently, Jesus had reiterated it:

> "You must love the LORD your God will all your heart, all your soul, and all your mind." This is the first and greatest commandment. A second is equally important: "Love your neighbor as yourself" (Matthew 22:37-39).

They would have also known that on the evening before He was crucified, Jesus gave new meaning to this verse in the upper-room conversation with His disciples:

> Now I am giving you a new commandment: Love each other. Just as I have loved you, you should love each other (John 13:34).

Although "love each other" doesn't sound new or very different from the pre-existing command to "love your neighbor as yourself," the disciples would soon come to understand the huge distinction. When Jesus gave the "new commandment," He was just hours away from giving His life in a sacrificial death for those disciples (and the rest of us). So when He said that the degree of their love should be "just as I have loved you," He was making clear that the standard of love was overwhelming self-sacrifice. Simply being nice or polite to each other is not the behavior that fulfills the "love your neighbor" standard. Christ wants us to love others with His sacrificial and self-giving love. That means we can't tell the poor people at church to go stand behind a pillar.

After laying out the "love your neighbor" law, James states that if you are guilty of paying special attention to the rich person (and thereby treating him more favorably than you treat the poor person), you are "committing a sin. You are guilty of breaking the law" (2:9). James doesn't hesitate to call a sin a sin.

Break One, Guilty of All

All of us have a natural tendency to minimize the significance of our sin. It doesn't seem as bad if we can rationalize that as insignificant. James didn't want his readers to think that the sin of their favoritism/discrimination was a minor offense to God. He didn't want them rationalizing, "I didn't discriminate against the poor person in church—I wasn't really mean to him. I was just extra nice to the rich guy. How bad can that be? I didn't kill anybody."

Some sins are more severe in their apparent consequences than others. Murder seems more egregious than gossip. But both are equal in that they evidence rebellion against God's principles. In the sense that God is holy and cannot tolerate sin, all sinful actions have the same impact—the person who commits the sin (whether heinous or seemingly insignificant) is guilty in the eyes of God, as Jesus taught:

> *If you ignore the least commandment and teach*
> *others to do the same, you will be called the least*
> *in the Kingdom of Heaven* (Matthew 5:19).

James reminds his readers that favoritism shown by them has the same consequences as other sins. He equates being guilty of murder with the sin of adultery. The one you commit (and the one you don't) doesn't make a difference from the standpoint of being guilty of sin. Breaking one of God's laws is the same as breaking all of them. There aren't degrees to our sinfulness based on a ranking of the sins we have committed. Breaking any one of them puts an obstacle between God and us. Consequently, you can't rationalize away sinful favoritism on the basis that it seems inconsequential.

Mercy Extended Means Mercy Received (2:13)

James brings out a final argument on the subject of favoritism/discrimination. He reminds his readers that they were shown mercy by God, so they should show mercy to others. And he goes one step further. He says that whether or not they will receive further mercy from God is dependent upon whether they show mercy to the poor.

James is not referring to God's mercy that saves a person for eternity. As will be discussed later, we don't earn our salvation by our good works, so it is not granted or withheld on the basis of whether we were kind to poor people. Rather, James is referring to God's use of mercy and blessings in our lives as we follow Him. Much like the children of

Israel, God blessed them when they followed His precepts, and He brought corrective events into their lives when they disobeyed His instructions. So, we are more apt to recognize God's blessings when we are imitating His character (including the way we treat the poor). If we aren't, it may be necessary for Him to withhold His blessings in order to get us focused on Him instead of ourselves.

It's About Mercy, Not Money

There is a false teaching called the "prosperity gospel" that is gaining in popularity. It promotes the misguided view that God wants every one of His followers to be rich in material possessions. The teaching basically states that if you give money to God, He will give more back to you.

This doctrine is wrong on many levels, but the purpose of mentioning it in our study of James is to clarify one of the foundational verses used in prosperity-gospel theology:

Give and you will receive. Your gift will return to you in full—pressed down, shaken together to make room for more, running over, and poured into your lap. The amount you give will determine the amount you get (Luke 6:38).

Those words spoken by Jesus, as quoted, seem to fit the position that God will give back to you more than you give to Him. But the verse is taken out of context when it is applied to money. It has nothing to do with money, and everything to do with mercy. The principle was stated by Jesus to describe how God extends mercy to us if we are merciful to others. Thus, when Jesus speaks of giving and receiving, He is referring to mercy: "If you give [mercy], you will receive [mercy]." Apparently the prosperity gospel proponents haven't noticed the verse that immediately precedes their favorite passage and establishes the context of mercy:

Do not judge others, and you will not be judged. Do not condemn others, or it will all come back against you. Forgive others, and you will be forgiven (Luke 6:37).

Study the Word

1. What are some deleterious results from showing favoritism? Are your answers any different if the favoritism takes place in the church?

2. How does the type of favoritism/discrimination that James wrote about contrast with God's characteristics?

3. Can you think of a time when you were treated as less-than-special at church?

4. Can you summarize the grounds upon which James argues that favoritism is wrong?

5. In today's culture, what group of people are we likely to show favoritism to? What group are we likely to ignore? What are the reasons we might prefer the one group and overlook the other? What are some ways in which we can avoid this natural tendency?

Only he who believes is obedient,
and only he who is obedient believes.

—*Dietrich Bonhoeffer*
(a leader of the underground Christian community
in Germany during World War II; executed on April 9, 1945,
in a concentration camp)

Is Your Faith All Talk?

Nothing infuriates James more than an empty, lifeless faith. His greatest concern is that people would think that they were saved when, in fact, they were not. To prevent people from fooling themselves, he would agree with Paul's entreaty:

> *Examine yourselves to see if your faith is genuine. Test yourselves* (2 Corinthians 13:5).

But examine ourselves for what? What should we be looking for to determine if our faith is genuine?

Not surprisingly, James has the answer. He has already given us some clues: loving your neighbor (2:8) and caring for the helpless (2:16). In other words, he wants to see some evidence that our faith is backed up by action. Whether you call it *works* or *deeds* or *fruit,* James says this is the proof of a genuine faith. And he goes so far as to say that a faith unaccompanied by such proof isn't faith at all.

We'll be getting into some deep theological concepts in this chapter, but don't let that divert you from the main focus—determining whether your faith is alive or dead.

Chapter 6

Have You Checked Your Spiritual Pulse?

James 2:14-26

What's Ahead

- Paul and James at Cross Purposes
- A Deedless Faith Is Dead Faith (2:14-20)
- Abraham, the Patriarch (2:21-24)
- Rahab, the Prostitute (2:25-26)

*E*arlier we mentioned that James is a very controversial book. At a quick glance, its teaching appears to contradict the writings of the apostle Paul who taught that salvation comes through faith alone. The passage we're studying in this chapter is where the apparent conflict arises. But we won't leave you hanging in suspense.

Here is what all the hubbub is about: Paul says we are saved by faith alone; James says faith without works can't save anyone. So who is right? Are works necessary for salvation or not?

Much of the apparent conflict is caused by the perspective on "works" (or deeds):

- *When Paul talks of* deeds, *he is using that term in a negative context.* He views *works* as doctrinal baggage that people feel they are obligated to perform in order to obtain God's forgiveness. For example, many of the Jewish Christians were telling the Gentile men that they had to follow the Jewish rite of circumcision in order to be saved. For Paul, works are an unnecessary burden.

- *When James talks of* deeds, *he is using that term in a positive context.* He views *works* as the good things people do when their lives have been transformed by the saving power of Jesus Christ. For example, attending to the needs of the widows and orphans would be a Christlike thing to do, which probably wouldn't happen without the influence of the Holy Spirit. For James, works are the natural result of a genuine faith.

With that background, let's examine what the Bible teaches about our justification through the work of Jesus Christ on the cross.

Paul and James at Cross Purposes

Before we get their alleged differences, let's look at what Paul and James both agree on:

- *We are separated from God because of our sins.* "Everyone has sinned; we all fall short of God's glorious standard" (Romans 3:23).

- *The penalty for our sins is eternal separation from God.* "The wages of sin is death" (Romans 6:23).

- *Good deeds won't get us to heaven:* "On judgment day many will say to me, 'Lord, Lord! We prophesied in your name and cast out demons in your name and performed many miracles in your name.' But I will reply, 'I never knew you. Get away from me, you who break God's laws'" (Matthew 7:22-23).

- *Nobody can come to God except through Jesus Christ.* "Jesus told him, 'I am the way, the truth, and the life. No one can come to the Father except through me'" (John 14:6).

- *Our sins are forgiven by Christ's death on the cross.* "God loved the world so much that he gave his one and only Son, so that everyone who believes in him will not perish but have eternal life" (John 3:16).

So we have the apostles Paul and James standing in agreement at the foot of the cross of Christ. Both agree that our salvation comes through surrendering our life to Christ in recognition that His sacrifice paid the penalty for our sin. By repenting of our sin and relinquishing our will to His, we are given eternal salvation. Once we are saved, we are justified (made righteous in God's sight). Everyone is in agreement so far.

But is more required? Paul says, "NO!" He contends that...

- *Salvation is a free gift:* "The free gift of God is eternal life through Christ Jesus our Lord" (Romans 6:23*).*

- *There is nothing we do to earn our salvation:* "Can we boast, then, that we have done anything to be accepted by God? No, because our acquittal is not based on obeying the law. It is based on faith. So we are made right with God through faith and not by obeying the law" (Romans 3:27-28).

- *We can't take credit in any way for our salvation:* "When people work, their wages are not a gift but something they have earned. But people are counted as righteous, not because of their work, but because of their faith in God who forgives sinners" (Romans 4:4-5).

- *Our salvation is not based on any good works that we may do:* "God saved you by his grace when you believed. And you can't take credit for this; it is a gift from God. Salvation is not a reward for the good things we have done, so none of us can boast about it" (Ephesians 2:8-9).

So where does James get off saying things like "can that kind of faith save anyone" (2:14) and "faith is dead without good works" (2:26)?

A Deedless Faith Is Dead Faith (2:14-20)

Once again, James tries to brace his readers for some upcoming stern words with a "dear brothers and sisters" reference. Why might his words be considered severe? Because he might be stepping on some toes when he talks about faith that is so shallow that it is actually dead. In fact, that is the key to understanding this entire passage. When James is talking about faith and works, he is using works as the indicator for whether a person's faith is vibrant or on life support.

James gives a hypothetical situation of a person who is destitute. The person with dead faith merely says, "Well, good luck with that." There is not a shred of Christ's love in this person that prompts any form of assistance. No offer of food. No offer of clothing. That person's faith is meaningless because it hasn't resulted in any Christlike behavior.

James emphasizes that a vibrant faith is always characterized by good deeds. This is not an alternative method for salvation—it is not a choice between faith or works. To make his point, James writes in a literary style called a *diatribe*, using an argumentative style. In verse 18, he makes his argument to an imaginary objector.

As James sees it, salvation is *not* a matter of:

- Faith *and* works. Salvation comes by faith alone.

- Faith *or* works. It is not either/or, because works is not an option for salvation.

- Faith *without* works. Although works never earn salvation, they are always present when the faith is legitimate and genuine.

For James, salvation is *always* a matter of faith *that* works.

True faith is internalized to the point where you are changed from the inside out. Faith is not authentic if it is merely intellectual assent to a doctrinal proposition. James uses Satan and the demons as an example. They believe in God. But their belief does not constitute saving faith. Their belief does not bring about a change of conduct consistent with surrender to God Almighty. Similarly, merely assenting that Jesus is the Son of God is not enough to bring salvation; a saving belief will bring about a change in a person's lifestyle. Thus, deeds don't bring salvation, but they reflect the depth and substance of a person's belief.

James isn't alone on this issue. No less an authority than Jesus Himself stated that actions reflect what is really in a person's heart. Using "fruit" as an analogy for deeds, Jesus said:

> *A good tree produces good fruit, and a bad tree produces bad fruit. A good tree can't produce bad fruit, and a bad tree can't produce good fruit. So every tree that does not produce good fruit is chopped down and thrown into the fire. Yes, just as you can identify a tree by its fruit, so you can identify people by their actions* (Matthew 7:17-20).

See? James didn't go out on a limb when he made this point.

Abraham, the Patriarch (2:21-24)

To illustrate his argument, James refers to Abraham. This was no stale historical reference for his readers—Abraham was a patriarch to the Jewish Christians. And they knew that God considered him righteous because of his belief in God:

> *If his good deeds had made him acceptable to God, he would have had something to boast about. But that was not God's way. For the Scriptures tell us, "Abraham believed God, and God counted him as righteous because of his faith"* (Romans 4:2-3).

James knows this story so well that he quoted the following verse from Genesis: "Abram believed the Lord, and the Lord declared him righteous because of his faith" (Genesis 15:6). And James and his readers are very aware that Abraham always acted on his faith, obeying God when called to relocated his family to an unknown land, and being willing to sacrifice his son at God's request.

It was Abraham's faith that made him righteous before God. His obedient actions were the natural outgrowth and expression of his mature faith.

Rahab, the Prostitute (2:25-26)

After Abraham, James moves ahead about 900 years and cites Rahab as an example. Her story is told in Joshua 2. She lived as a prostitute in the pagan city of Jericho. When the Israelites sent a reconnaissance team to the city prior to attacking it, Rahab hid the Jewish spies from the king. She had heard the stories of how the God of the Israelites had protected them when they had escaped from Egypt, and she was familiar with the stories of God's miraculous provision for them while they were in the wilderness. She not only believed in God's existence, but she trusted in Him. Accordingly, she was willing to risk being exposed as a traitor in order to help the Israelite spies escape the city. As the result of her faith—as manifested by her actions—God spared her life when the city of Jericho was attacked by the Israelites.

In the book of Hebrews, chapter 11 lists a number of people from the Old Testament who are famous for outward conduct that displayed their inner faith. Even though she was a non-Jew and a prostitute, Rahab made the list along with the superstars of the Jewish faith:

> *It was by faith that Rahab the prostitute was not*
> *destroyed with the people in her city who refused*
> *to obey God. For she had given a friendly welcome*
> *to the spies* (Hebrews 11:31).

Interestingly, Rahab didn't do any of the things we typically associate with a person of faith. Most likely, she didn't go to church, she didn't have a daily devotional reading regime, and she didn't have a prayer time. Her knowledge of God was rudimentary at best. She simply had heard about God, and she believed in Him. Her faith in Him—as evidenced by her actions—was authentic enough for God to grant righteousness to her.

James concludes this discussion by presenting the converse of what he has been saying: Just as a vital faith is revealed by action, inaction reveals a faith that is dead. Does he mean that such a faith was alive at one time but subsequently died? No, he is referring to a faith that never existed in the first place. A dead faith is one where the person merely professed belief in Christ but never had any substance behind it. James wants his readers to compare their faith to that of Abraham and Rahab. Does their faith produce action based on obedience to God's direction, or is it dead? The answer reveals whether you have faith at all.

Did Paul Agree with James?

He sure did. Most of the time he was arguing against people who wanted to *add* works as a prerequisite for salvation (thus, he is famous for the "faith alone" slogan). But Paul firmly believed that a vibrant faith would result in good deeds, and that a faith without accompanying works was useless.

When we place our faith in Christ Jesus, there is no benefit in being circumcised or being uncircumcised. What is important is faith expressing itself in love (Galatians 5:6).

"Expressing itself in love" is exactly the kind of result James expects to see in a person whose faith is genuine.

■ ■ ■

Study the Word

1. Why do some people believe that the teachings of Paul about faith are in conflict with the position held by James? How are the positions of the two reconciled?

2. What are the kinds of results that James expects to see from someone who has a vibrant faith? What is the evidence that someone's faith is lifeless?

3. How do 1 John 3:10 and 1 John 3:17-19 relate to what James has been talking about?

4. Read Matthew 25:31-46 and explain how it relates the faith/works discussion.

5. What is wrong with the belief in God held by Satan and his demons? Is there a difference between their belief in God and James's faith in God?

> The control of the tongue is more than an evidence
> of spiritual maturity; it is the means to it.
>
> —J.A. Motyer

Watch Your Talk

Controlling our conversation is one of James's hot buttons. He addresses this subject in every chapter of his epistle. Remember the "be slow to speak" from 1:19, the "control your tongue" from 1:26, and the "whatever you say" in 2:12. (And we'll get to the subject again in 4:11 and 5:12.) But the present passage, 3:1-12, represents his most extensive discussion of the topic.

Why is James so intent on this subject? Because he understands the damage that our words cause, both to ourselves and others. And he doesn't want us to be misled—although the tongue is small in size, it wields tremendous power and can do massive damage.

On a personal level, we're apt to minimize and underestimate the sins we commit by our conversation. After all, gossip seems relatively harmless compared to murder, adultery, and theft. And that's another reason why James wants to alert us to the importance of monitoring what we say. As he points out, our tongue has the ability to cause damage that is subtle but grievous.

Chapter 7

Has Your Tongue Gone Wild?

James 3:1-12

*W*hat's *A*head

- A Warning for Teachers (3:1)
- Controlling Horses and Ships (3:2-5a)
- Battling the Fire and Taming the Beast (3:5b-8)
- Blessings and Curses (3:9-12)

*A*s we begin James 3, we've just finished a heavy discussion in which James has said that works, not words, are the true indicator of a person's faith. Now he shifts his emphasis, and in so doing, he indicates that words are not altogether irrelevant. Although they aren't an accurate indicator of genuine faith among those who only "talk the walk," our words do play a significant role in our spiritual life.

As we'll see in this study, James is emphatic about controlling our words because...

- *They have the power to destroy:* "Your tongue cuts like a sharp razor" (Psalm 52:2).
- *They have the power to heal:* "Some people make cutting remarks, but the words of the wise bring healing" (Proverbs 12:18).

- *They reflect the true sentiments in a person's heart:* "Evil words come from an evil heart and defile the man who says them" (Matthew 15:18 TLB).

- *They must be monitored and controlled at all times so as to avoid problems:* "If you want to enjoy life and see many happy days, keep your tongue from speaking evil and your lips from telling lies" (1 Peter 3:10).

A Warning for Teachers (3:1)

Everyone is going to fall within the coverage of James's scolding on the subject of speech, but he eases into it by targeting a smaller group he's in himself. To understand his reference to "teachers," it might be helpful to know that a custom in local synagogues allowed random members of the congregation (and even visitors) to stand up and teach at the *Shabbat* (the Saturday Sabbath service). Both Jesus and Paul took advantage of this custom in their travels. Bible scholars believe that James had this tradition in mind when he cautioned his readers about being "teachers."

Imagine what things would be like in your own church if anyone could walk up to the microphone and preach a mini-sermon. It is likely that some of the volunteers would speak from a knowledgeable and informed background. But others might be voicing their own opinions (not God's); some might be speaking out of resentment or anger; others might be doing it all for show.

Paul mentions that teaching is one of the special abilities bestowed by the Holy Spirit:

> *God has given us different gifts for doing certain things well. So if God has given you the ability to prophesy, speak out with as much faith as God has given you. If your gift is serving others,*

serve them well. If you are a teacher, teach well
(Romans 12:6-7).

James is not trying to discourage people from speaking
if they have the spiritual gift of teaching. He is more concerned about those who are ignorant or careless with regard
to interpreting the Word of God. Anyone who teaches
assumes a great deal of responsibility. The teachers will be
held to a stricter degree of accountability. (This is the type
of judgment to which James refers, not judgment relating
to eternal damnation.)

Whether we are teachers or not, we should be students
of the Scripture so that 1) we are not led astray by someone
who is teaching false doctrine, and 2) we don't mislead
others when we do speak about spiritual matters.

> *Work hard so you can present yourself to God and
> receive his approval. Be a good worker, one who does
> not need to be ashamed and who correctly explains
> the word of truth. Avoid worthless, foolish talk that
> only leads to more godless behavior. This kind of
> talk spreads like cancer* (2 Timothy 2:15-17).

Controlling Horses and Ships (3:2-5a)

James acknowledges that none of us is perfect. We all
mess up from time to time. But it will happen less often if
we learn to discipline our tongue and exhibit some control
over our conversations.

From an anatomical perspective, the tongue is a small
part of our bodies. Yet it can cause disproportionately large
amounts of damage. James uses two analogies to illustrate:

- *A horse is controlled by a bit:* A horse may weigh 1500
  pounds, yet it can be controlled by a one-pound

piece of metal hardware placed in its mouth. With small tugs on the bit, the rider can turn a powerful horse in either direction, or bring a galloping stallion to a complete stop.

- *A ship is controlled by a rudder:* The direction of a huge ocean liner is set by its diminutive rudder. The slightest change in the position of the rudder will change the heading, either setting the course toward its destination or steering it off course.

Similarly, the tongue is a small member of our bodies, but it has the potential to cause great harm or great good:

> *Gentle words are a tree of life; a deceitful tongue crushes the spirit* (Proverbs 15:4).

Given the mouth's potential for abuse, it might be better to keep it closed than to risk unintended damage.

> *Watch your tongue and keep your mouth shut, and you will stay out of trouble* (Proverbs 21:23).

Battling the Fire and Taming the Beast (3:5b-8)

We have all heard of forest fires that are started by a careless camper. It could all begin with a single match. Something so small has the capacity to cause so much damage. James compares the ravages of a forest fire to the damage of a tongue on the loose. An unguarded word spoken in anger, or an insult slung in retribution, or a lie told carelessly or in spite—these are the matches that can ignite a raging inferno with disastrous consequences.

> *The lying tongue tumbles into trouble* (Proverbs 17:20).

James states that the tongue has such great potential for harm because it is full of wickedness. Of course, the wickedness doesn't originate in your mouth. It comes from a place deeper inside of you: your heart. Christ taught that all of our sin originates there:

> *From the heart come evil thoughts, murder, adultery, all sexual immorality, theft, lying, and slander. These are what defile you* (Matthew 15:19-20).

When he says that the tongue can be set on fire by hell itself, James is referring to Satan. We shouldn't be surprised that Satan can instigate circumstances that prompt us to cause damage with our speech if we do not control our tongue. When our heart and our tongue are uncontrolled, the results are dangerous:

> *Their talk is foul, like the stench from an open grave. Their tongues are filled with lies. Snake venom drips from their lips. Their mouths are full of cursing and bitterness* (Romans 3:13-14).

Ironically, humans can tame all sorts of wild animals, but not their tongues. It is futile because our speech reflects what is in our hearts. If our hearts are unregenerate, then our speech will reflect the depravity of our souls.

> *You love to destroy others with your words, you liar!* (Psalm 52:4).

Is Controlling Your Tongue an Exercise in Futility?

When James says no one can tame the tongue, he means no one under their own power. But if you have Christ in your life, then there is hope. A transformed soul can lead to reformed conversation. James would be in full agreement with Paul when he said,

Since you have been raised to new life with Christ...think about the things of heaven...So put to death the sinful, earthly things lurking within you. Have nothing to do with sexual immorality, impurity, lust, and evil desires...You used to do them when your life was still part of this world. But now is the time to get rid of anger, rage, malicious behavior, slander, and dirty language. Don't lie to each other, for you have stripped off your old sinful nature and all its wicked deeds. Put on your new nature, and be renewed as you learn to know your Creator and become like him (Colossians 3:1-10).

You are a new creation as the result of your salvation through Christ. With that comes the ability to change your speech habits through the power of the Holy Spirit. It takes self-control and a commitment to speak only in a way that is pleasing to God.

I said to myself, "I will watch what I do and not sin in what I say. I will hold my tongue when the ungodly are around me" (Psalm 39:1).

Blessings and Curses (3:9-12)

Interestingly, our tongue can be schizophrenic. Sometimes it speaks words that are kind, while other times its output is vile.

The tongue can bring death of life; those who love to talk will reap the consequences (Proverbs 18:21).

Our voice is best served when it is used for the purpose of praising God:

> *I will proclaim your justice, and I will praise you all day long* (Psalm 35:28).

But unfortunately, we are often guilty of using it to disrespect others, all of whom are valued and loved by God:

> *Their tongues shoot lies like poisoned arrows. They speak friendly words to their neighbors while scheming in their heart to kill them* (Jeremiah 9:8).

Though James mentions "curses," he isn't limiting his comments to blasphemy, profanity, and obscenities. We must recognize that it is wholly inappropriate for us, as Christians, to engage in any type of slander, gossip, lies, and other verbal abuse. If our entire bodies are dedicated to God (see Romans 12:1), then we shouldn't be participating with any part of our bodies in behavior that is contrary to His nature.

James gives three illustrations to emphasize that using our voice to utter offensive statements is contrary to our new nature as Christians:

- An underground spring wouldn't produce both bitter water as well as fresh water;
- a fig tree wouldn't produce olives, and a grapevine wouldn't produce figs; and
- fresh water can't be drawn from a pond of salt water.

Just as these outcomes would be impossible, it should be equally inconceivable that bad words would emanate from the mouth of a child of God. Instead of having a tongue that wags out both curses and blessings, we should strive to use it only to the glory of God.

> *Let your conversation be gracious and attractive so that you will have the right response for everyone* (Colossians 4:6).

*W*hat *D*oes *G*od *T*hink of *A*ll of *T*his?

Do you wonder if these slips of the tongue (such as lying, gossip, and harmful comments) bother God as much as they bother James? Is he blowing this out of proportion? Hardly.

Check this "Top Seven Things That God Hates" list that was compiled by King Solomon, the wisest man who ever lived:

> *There are six things the LORD hates—no, seven things he detests: haughty eyes, a lying tongue, hands that kill the innocent, a heart that plots evil, feet that race to do wrong, a false witness who pours out lies, a person who sows discord in a family* (Proverbs 6:16-19).

The tongue is involved in three out of seven of the things that God hates. James apparently knows what he is talking about.

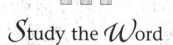

*S*tudy the *W*ord

1. Why is it so difficult for us to control what we say?

2. Do you agree with James that no one can tame their tongue? James wants us to do so through the power of the Holy Spirit, but how does that happen at a practical level?

3. Can you think of an instance in which terrible hurt was caused by a careless comment spoken by you or about you?

4. Review the analogies James uses in his treatise on the tongue. What are some other analogies that illustrate the tongue's potential for damage? Is there one analogy in particular (either James's or your own) that is especially effective in motivating you to be more careful with your words?

5. What practical steps are you going to implement to make sure your speech is reflective of Christ's character?

We have here again what may be described as the central thought of this epistle [James], that where religion [the Gospel] has real saving hold of a mind and heart, it cannot from its nature but power- fully influence the outward life; and that the more a Christian has of true wisdom and spiritual knowl- edge, the more manifestly will his life at all points be governed by his religion [faith]. Talk of ortho- doxy and Christian experience, however fluent and animated and clever, does not of itself prove wisdom; the really wise man will "show his work."

—Robert Johnstone

Put Your Wisdom to the Test

Television game shows have been in vogue as long as tele- vision sets have been around. There is something intriguing about testing whether you have the multiple choice acumen to be a millionaire, can guess your way into a deal or no deal, are smarter than a fifth-grader, or can respond with a ques- tion to an answer posed by Alex Trebek.

Are you ready to play a game proposed by James? He wants to know whether you are choosing "Human Wisdom" or "God's Wisdom." James will be the host, but God will be the judge. Don't bother answering aloud. Any answer you give verbally will be ignored because it is too easy for people to claim they have God's wisdom when they really don't. The true answer will be determined by whether you have been living a godly lifestyle.

This chapter will require that you examine your behavior, your attitudes, and your motivations. Get ready to play. The theme music is starting to swell.

Chapter 8

Which Wisdom Do You Choose?

James 3:13-18

---

*W*hat's *A*head

- ▪ Got Wisdom? (3:13)
- ▪ Human Wisdom (3:14-16)
- ▪ God's Wisdom (3:17-18)

*I*t's not a broken record. It's not repetition ad nauseam. Consider it positive reinforcement of a principle that is otherwise counterintuitive: If you really are committed to faith in Christ, then there will be some outward evidence to prove it.

Many people claim to be followers of Christ, but if Christianity were against the law, there wouldn't be enough evidence to convict them. James has said that the true Christians—those who have a genuine faith—will be obvious by...

- • their impartiality to both the rich and the poor (2:1-13);
- • the good deeds and righteous acts they do (2:14-26); and
- • the way in which they control their tongue (3:1-12).

But that's not all. In the present passage James adds another telltale sign to the list: wisdom. As he'll explain, there are two kinds of wisdom: one is a faulty and perverted wisdom devised by humanity; the other is exemplary wisdom that comes from God. The lifestyles based on these alternative foundations are so drastically opposed to each other that the respective source is readily apparent. It doesn't take a theologian to ascertain which type of wisdom a person is relying upon. All that is necessary is an examination of the consequences that have arisen from the person's decisions and choices.

Before we wade into this chapter's passage, let's clarify what the Bible is talking about when it refers to *wisdom*. The ancient Greek and Roman usage of the term placed more emphasis on the intellectual aspect of gaining knowledge. The Old Testament references to wisdom, on the other hand, point to a blend of factual knowledge with its application in the context of God's truth. Thus, the Bible makes a distinction between intelligence and wisdom. *Knowledge* (smarts) has merit, to be sure, but *wisdom* (insight) governs the application of the knowledge. These are companion virtues: intelligence and wisdom. The former has far less value without the latter. For this reason, you often see these companion terms used in combination, as Moses did when he announced God's laws to the Israelites:

> *I now teach you these decrees and regulations...so that you may obey them in the land you are about to enter and occupy. Obey them completely, and you will display your wisdom and intelligence among the surrounding nations* (Deuteronomy 4:5-6).

When used in the Bible, *knowledge* and *intelligence* don't usually refer to the mere possession of textbook facts.

Instead, *knowledge* and *intelligence* are equated with understanding God's principles. (In other words, the most important things for you to know are things about God.) So, the knowledge/wisdom combination is often described in terms of *understanding* (knowledge of God and His principles) and *wisdom* (good judgment in applying that understanding to the circumstances of life).

> *Choose some well-respected men from each tribe who are known for their wisdom and understanding, and I will appoint them as your leaders* (Deuteronomy 1:13).

The Bible is consistent throughout in placing a high value on wisdom (the ability to apply God's truth to life's circumstances). The richest depository on this subject is the book of Proverbs. It is not surprising that Proverbs contains a good explanation of the combination of understanding God's truth and having the wisdom to apply it in real-life situations:

> *My child, listen to what I say and treasure my commands. Tune your ears to wisdom, and concentrate on understanding. Cry out for insight, and ask for understanding. Search for them as you would for silver; seek them like hidden treasures. Then you will understand what it means to fear the LORD, and you will gain knowledge of God. For the LORD grants wisdom! From his mouth come knowledge and understanding. He grants a treasure of common sense to the honest. He is a shield to those who walk with integrity. He guards the paths of the just and protects those who are faithful to him. Then you will understand what is right, just, and fair, and you will find the right*

way to go. For wisdom will enter your heart, and
knowledge will fill you with joy. Wise choices will
watch over you. Understanding will keep you safe
(Proverbs 2:1-11).

Finally, as we prepare to dissect what James has written about wisdom, we need to realize the priority that God places on it. If we wish to live a spiritually successful life, then wisdom is an absolute necessity:

Getting wisdom is the wisest thing you can do!
And whatever else you do, develop good judgment
(Proverbs 4:7).

Because wisdom is the application of God's principles to the circumstances of life, then implicit in the above exhortation is the companion requirement that we must have an understanding of God's character and precepts.

Okay, that's your prerequisite orientation. Now, let's see what James has to say about all of this.

Got Wisdom? (3:13)

James begins with a reference to the foundational combination of understanding and wisdom. He implies that this combination is most likely to produce the kind of exemplary behavior that is a testament to a vibrant faith in God. Thus, at the outset of this discussion, he describes the standard that should be our target.

Although he doesn't specifically mention them, it seems James has certain people in mind as he begins this passage. These are not people whose examples James wants us to emulate. (And maybe that is why he doesn't expressly refer to them.) Rather, they are the kind who exhibit the earthly wisdom he will soon be condemning. Apparently there were people of this ilk throughout the churches to whom James was writing. They thought they were wise (when they really weren't), and they bragged about it. In contrast to the arrogance they displayed, James wants us to realize that a life of understanding and applying God's truth is characterized by gentleness and humility.

Human Wisdom (3:14-16)

James still doesn't name the people to whom he made an indirect reference in 3:13, but now his remarks about them are more explicit. In these three verses, James explains that there is a false wisdom that is promoted by people who are void of godly character. Since they lack understanding of who God is and are not influenced by Him, they are incapable of teaching about godly wisdom. Consequently, anything they promote is simply human thinking and lacks spiritual substance. As a result, their teaching is flawed.

Regarding human wisdom—as he will do in his discussion of God's wisdom—James talks about the *traits* and the *results*.

The Traits of Human Wisdom

Jealousy and selfish ambition spring from wisdom rooted in the context of humanity. In other words, the natural characteristics will be self-interest (self-centeredness) and envy (selfishly wanting what others have). These don't come from God, so any teaching that promotes them must be false. If they don't come from God, they are earthly and unspiritual. They then must find their root in Satan.

The Results of Human Wisdom

What is the product of rampant jealousy and selfishness? James explains that disorder and evil are the result. His reference to "evil" is meant to convey the picture of evil practices within the Christian community. James has already told us that true faith results in good deeds. Here he is making the converse point: False faith results in evil deeds.

God's Wisdom (3:17-18)

James now moves to the opposite of human wisdom—God's wisdom. Again, he identifies both traits and results found in divine wisdom.

The Traits of God's Wisdom

James identifies eight characteristics that arise from a life based in God's wisdom:

- *Purity:* A heart that is pure is considered holy and undefiled. Christ said that "God blesses those whose hearts are pure, for they will see God" (Matthew 5:8). And without a pure heart, your fellowship with Him is cut off: "Those who are not holy will not see the Lord" (Hebrews 12:14).

- *Peacefulness:* In the application of God's wisdom, people don't attempt to advance their own selfish agenda. Their humility creates an atmosphere of tranquility. As Jesus said, "God blesses those who work for peace, for they will be called the children of God" (Matthew 5:9).

- *Gentleness:* It doesn't sound very manly, does it? But don't get the impression that this characteristic is all about softness and fragility. Actually, it should be equated with fairness and courtesy and the ability to endure persecution. This is the trait the apostle Paul taught would be useful in confrontational situations: "A servant of the Lord must not quarrel but must be kind to everyone, be able to teach, and be patient with difficult people. They gently instruct those who oppose the truth" (2 Timothy 2:24-25).

- *Reasonableness:* A person with this characteristic can understand the opposite side of an argument. There is no insistence on "doing it my way." The sake of peace in the community prevails over a personal agenda. A reasonable person is teachable and willing to make changes against his or her own preference when the alternative doesn't jeopardize the desired outcome.

- *Mercy:* A merciful spirit does more than just forgive a wrong that has been suffered. It goes beyond forgiveness to extend additional graciousness and courtesy to the wrongdoer. God Himself is the best example of mercy, for He has forgiven our sins, and He additionally has made a plan for us to become His children and spend eternity in His fellowship. Christ underscored the virtue of mercy in the Sermon on the Mount: "God blesses those who are merciful, for they will be shown mercy" (Matthew 5:7).

- *Good deeds:* This should come as no surprise to you. Of course James will insist that good deeds are the characteristic of a life genuinely rooted in God's principles.

- *Impartiality:* Does this remind you of James's teaching in 2:2-7, when he criticized favoritism toward the rich with resulting discrimination to the poor? There will be none of that if godly wisdom is present.

- *Sincerity:* There is no place for hypocrisy in God's paradigm. Christ frequently made this crystal clear when He chastised the Pharisees for their two-facedness, such as when he said, "Hypocrites! For you are like whitewashed tombs—beautiful on the outside but filled on the inside with dead people's bones and all sorts of impurity. Outwardly you look like righteous people, but inwardly your hearts are filled with hypocrisy and lawlessness" (Matthew 23:27-28).

These traits produce an atmosphere of peace within the Christian community. This type of peace does not mean that people need to concede their convictions for the sake of tranquility, but rather suggest that they can live harmoniously and wisely even though their opinions may differ.

James ends the discussion of wisdom by explaining the beneficial cycle that comes from a life lived in accordance with God's principles: Those who are pursuing faith are sowing seeds of righteousness that produce a harvest of goodness.

Paul Would Say "Amen" to All of This

James wasn't the only New Testament epistle writer who knew a thing or two about wisdom. If Paul were allowed to chime in on this wisdom dialogue, he would want to contribute the following thoughts:

- According to God's plan, the understanding of Him and His wisdom can be found in Jesus Christ.

  I want them to have complete confidence that they understand God's mysterious plan, which is Christ himself. In him lie hidden all the treasures of wisdom and knowledge (Colossians 2:2-3).

- James correctly states that there is a huge distinction between God's wisdom and human wisdom. But Paul additionally points out that earthly wisdom is so far off kilter that it considers the ways of God to be foolish:

To those called by God to salvation, both Jews and Gentiles, Christ is the power of God and the wisdom of God. This foolish plan of God is wiser than the wisest of human plans, and God's weakness is stronger than the greatest of human strength...God chose things the world considers foolish in order to shame those who think they are wise. And he chose those who are powerless to shame those who are powerful. God chose things despised by the world, things counted as nothing at all, and used them to bring to nothing what the world considers important As a result, no one can ever boast in the presence of God (1 Corinthians 1:24-29).

- Even the best Christianity 101® Bible study on James won't be good enough to allow you to grasp the incomprehensible magnitude of God's wisdom:

Oh, how great are God's riches and wisdom and knowledge! How impossible it is for us to understand his decisions and his methods! "For who can know the LORD's thoughts? Who knows enough to give him advice?"...For everything comes from him and exists by his power and is intended for his glory (Romans 11:33-36).

◼ ◼ ◼

Study the Word

1. How would James define *knowledge* and *wisdom?* How would he distinguish these words from each other?

2. How does James define and distinguish "God's wisdom" from "human wisdom"?

3. Describe an environment that is pervaded by human wisdom. How is the atmosphere different if it is rooted in God's wisdom?

4. Think of a situation in your experience when there was a monumental disagreement between two people. Using that factual situation as a hypothetical scenario, how might the conflict play out under principles of earthly wisdom? What would the resolution look like using God's wisdom?

5. How, practically, can we transition from operating under human wisdom to a mind-set that relies on God's wisdom? What are the steps that we must take?

I have often wondered that persons who make
boast of professing the Christian religion—namely
love, joy, peace, temperance, and charity to all
men—should quarrel with such rancorous animosity,
and display daily towards one another such bitter
hatred, that this, rather than the virtues which they
profess, is the readiest criteria of their faith.

—*Spinoza*
(seventeenth-century Jewish philosopher)

It Isn't As Easy As It Looks

In theory and on paper, living the Christian life seems like a manageable proposition. *Love God with all your heart, mind, and soul.* Check. *Love your neighbor as yourself.* Check. How tough can that be?

As it turns out, pretty difficult. If you've been a Christian for a long time, you already know this. If you are new to Christianity, we're sorry to disillusion you. But the harsh reality is, Christians struggle to live a life that pleases God. We are engaged in a constant battle to do things that are pleasing to God while refraining from actions that disappoint Him.

We're at war—with ourselves! We are our own worst enemy, or more precisely, our old sin nature is our archenemy. These struggles within ourselves spill over into quarrels with others and put us at odds with God. And that is just the opposite of how we want things to be.

In this chapter, we'll study James's take on this problem. (See—we told you that he was interested in getting down to the practical aspects of the Christian life.)

Chapter 9

Are Your Motivations Pulling You Away from God?

James 4:1-10

What's Ahead

- The Battle Rages (4:1-3)
- Enemies with God (4:4-6)
- Drawing Close to God (4:7-10)

*L*ook back at the passage we just studied. Do you remember James's references to bitter jealousy and selfish ambition (3:14)—and disorder and evil (3:16)? These are the characteristics and consequences of life based on human wisdom. This is not the target we are shooting for. But it is the reality in which many of us live.

In the present passage James steps away from the discussion of God's wisdom vs. human wisdom and gets more personal. In fact, he gets to the nitty-gritty of Christian life—the inner struggle that so often besets us, with the result that God seems distant from us. But not to worry. In his practical fashion, James gives not only an accurate assessment of the problem, but he also describes the solution.

The Battle Rages (4:1-3)

James begins the discussion by broaching the subject of quarrels and infighting in the Christian community.

Apparently it was a common occurrence for members in various local congregations to be fighting with each other. Disputes probably raged over doctrinal issues, power struggles, and petty grievances.

The apostle Paul noticed the same problem as he traveled among those early Christian churches. Just like James, Paul felt compelled to correct this situation by making mention of it:

> *I appeal to you, dear brothers and sisters, by the authority of the Lord Jesus Christ, to live in harmony with each other. Let there be no divisions in the church. Rather, be of one mind, united in thought and purpose* (1 Corinthians 1:10).

Still Fighting After All These Years

Almost 2000 years have gone by and, unfortunately, Christians haven't matured much beyond this point. Church members are still fighting with each other over doctrinal issues, power struggles, and petty grievances. This is an immense tragedy because the impression we're making on the world is that we are petty and argumentative—so much so that we can't even get along with ourselves. This is exactly the opposite of the impression Christ wants us to make. This is how He described the ideal reputation for his followers:

> *Your love for one another will prove to the world that you are my disciples* (John 13:35).

By the way, if we lack the love we should have for other Christians, then we aren't exhibiting the goodness that should naturally accompany our faith. We don't need to remind you what James says about a faith that is without good deeds. (This is getting way too personal for some of us, isn't it?)

While our gut reaction may be to blame the strife in the church on the other guy, James beats us to the punch by laying the blame on us. By asking a rhetorical question that has a resounding "Yes!" as its answer, James lays the blame on the evil desires that reside within us. Although we might not like his diagnosis, it makes sense: If we are filled with turmoil and not at peace with God, it is logical that we might be at odds with other members of His family.

James proceeds to identify several struggles that rage within us. As we review them, notice how each is rooted in the kind of bitter jealousy and selfish ambition that is characteristic of human wisdom.

We Want but We Don't Have, So We Kill to Get It

James doesn't even have to give specifics. We all struggle with a strong desire for something. It may be for physical pleasure, material wealth, social status, recognition, prestige, power, or something else. So far, we can agree with James. But isn't he exaggerating a bit when he says we will kill to obtain the things we lust for?

Within his intended context, James uses the correct word. He doesn't mean we would go so far as to actually commit murder, but we might be guilty of engaging in conduct that is destructive to ourselves and others. Our desire for what we don't have, if not controlled, might lead us to commit sins that leave a trail of dead or injured bodies behind us, figuratively speaking.

We Want What Others Have, So We Fight to Take It Away

Oftentimes our fights and disputes stem from envy for something we want, something possessed by someone else.

Maybe we spread rumors about the person who got the job promotion we wanted. Maybe we backstab an ex-spouse in the hope of changing child-custody arrangements. Maybe we despise someone who has had an easy life while ours has always been tough. Or, it might simply be resentment directed toward someone who has happiness that is missing in our own lives.

We Want, but We Don't Ask for It

Often we are so self-centered that it does not even occur to us to ask God for what we want. Perhaps we are so self-deluded that we believe we're capable of obtaining what we desire under our own power and devices. Thus, we don't bother asking God because we can take care of ourselves, we think.

When We Ask for it, We Don't Get It

Sooner or later, we recognize the futility of our own efforts, and in desperation we turn to God. But our prayers go unanswered. Our self-centered instinct tells us that God is intentionally trying to frustrate us. This gives us one more thing to be mad about. In reality, our prayers are being answered, but the answer is "No" because we are praying with selfish motives. When God withholds something we want, He has our best interests in mind. He knows better than we whether something we've asked for will be beneficial or harmful.

Enemies with God (4:4-6)

James doesn't call his hearers "adulterers" merely for shock value. That is exactly what his readers are if they abandoned the love of God in favor of a love for what the world has to offer. You can either love God or the world.

It is an either/or proposition. To lust after what the world offers is to turn your back on God:

> *Do not love this world nor the things it offers you, for when you love the world, you do not have the love of the Father in you. For the world offers only a craving for physical pleasure, a craving for everything we see, and pride in our achievements and possessions. These are not from the Father, but are from this world* (1 John 2:15-16).

Apparently James wants the "if you love the world, then you are the enemy of God" principle to sink in, because he says it twice in a row. But even though we constantly turn our backs on God, He continues to pursue an intimate fellowship with us. In fact, James says that God is jealous over His relationship with us. Doesn't it seem odd that James would attribute *jealousy* to God? Isn't our jealousy one of the reasons we've been sucked into human wisdom?

When James speaks of God's jealousy for us, he is referring to God's righteous concern for our spiritual well-being. In the same manner that parents want what is best for their child (whether the kid realizes it or not), so too does God want what is best for us. He contends for our soul and our relationship with Him. He watches over us and does not want us to damage ourselves by ignoring Him.

Up to this point, James has pounded on his readers pretty good. Figuring he might have succeeded in tenderizing their hearts, now he gives them hope that it is not too late to turn back to God. His grace is still available to them. His strength is capable of pulling them out of the snares of their evil desires. Of course, there will need to be repentance and humility on their part because God does not extend His grace to those who maintain an arrogant and rebellious attitude.

Drawing Close to God (4:7-10)

In these four verses, James tells his Christian readers how they can rid themselves of the spiritually detrimental entanglements that accompany human wisdom. But he must also be mindful that some of his readers are not Christians at all. If they have no evidence of good deeds in their life, then their so-called faith may be dead and useless. Thus, his steps for spiritual reconciliation with God apply equally to the person who is approaching Christ for the first time, as well as to the longtime Christian who has temporarily drifted away from God.

Humble Yourself

Whether you are approaching God for salvation or returning to Him, He must be approached in humility. Our relationship with God needs to be one of submission to His holiness and to His authority. Holding on to our rights, privileges, and position makes sense in the paradigm of human wisdom. In God's realm, however, you gain your life only when you willingly relinquish your ownership of it to Christ:

> *If you refuse to take up your cross and follow me, you are not worthy of being mine. If you cling to your life, you will lose it; but if you give up your life for me, you will find it* (Matthew 10:38-39).

God can't be your Savior if you don't submit to Him as Lord.

Resist the Devil

Although we belong to God, we still live in a world in which Satan, for the time being, runs rampant.

> *We know that we are children of God and that the world around us is under the control of the evil one* (1 John 5:19).

Submitting to God will not insulate us from the attacks of Satan. In fact, he will be more intent on ensnaring us in sin as we become more serious about our faith. (He doesn't need to waste his effort on Christians whose faith is ineffectual and unproductive.) But through the Holy Spirit we are empowered to resist Satan, and James states the promise that Satan will flee from us if we do so.

Draw Close to God

James wants us to enter into and enjoy a close personal relationship with God. This is not just a "see you next Sunday" kind of friendship. Rather, it involves constant conversation, honest confession, and true reverence and worship. Don't miss the amazing promise in this verse: If we draw near to God, He *will* draw near to us. But remember that God is a perfect gentleman. He won't force the relationship. He will approach us only when we have turned to Him.

> *Let us come boldly to the throne of our gracious God. There we will receive his mercy, and we will find grace to help us when we need it most...Let us go right into the presence of God with sincere hearts fully trusting him* (Hebrews 4:16; 10:22).

Purify Your Heart and Hands

Jewish priests went through a ceremonial procedure

before they offered sacrifices. The tradition was symbolic of the cleansing and purification we need to have accomplished in our hearts when we enter God's presence. By making reference to this symbolism that was familiar to his readers, James is telling us to confess our sins so that the condition of our heart is acceptable before the Lord.

> *Who may stand in his holy place? Only those whose hands and hearts are pure* (Psalm 24:3-4).

Be Sorrowful

At first glance, you might think that James is opposed to having any fun. Verse 4:9 certainly seems like he is suggesting that Christians should be morose. Instead, he is telling us to seriously consider the gravity of our former condemnation and set aside the flippant and trivial distractions of life. We will appreciate God's mercy all the more when we reflect on the shame of our former conduct.

What is the result if you take these steps? James says that your fellowship with God will be restored. Once again you can enjoy the intimacy of a personal relationship with Him. Acknowledging your dependence on Him will set you free of the evil entanglements that ensnared you in the past and made your life difficult.

◻ ◻ ◻

Study the Word

1. If Christ was all about love, how come some of His followers have such a difficult time showing it to each other?

2. What does James identify as the underlying cause of contentious relationships between Christians?

3. What causes the breakdown of our fellowship with God?

4. Explain the process James identifies for restoring our relationship with God. Which part of the process would be the easiest for you? Which would be the most difficult?

5. What does James mean when he says that God is jealous for us?

What James encourages is not the constant verbalization of the formula "If the Lord wills," which can easily become a glib and meaningless recitation, but a sincere appreciation for God's control of affairs and for his specific will for us.

—*Douglas J. Moo*

Sheer Arrogance

The people to whom James was writing must have been an arrogant bunch. Already in our study we have seen James make repeated references to their pride and self-centeredness. Now, in this next passage, we deal again with this moral failing. This time, however, James pinpoints their arrogance as it is displayed in forms of slander, judging others, and presuming to make plans independent of God's involvement.

As much as we might like to think that these were problems unique to the Jewish Christian community in the first-century Mediterranean world, we can't avoid the conviction that we are guilty of the same spiritual maladies. We slander our Christian brothers and sister when we condemn them for failing to meet our expectations; we judge the level of their spiritual commitment, when this is a sacred matter that is between them and the Lord; and we are so proud of our independence that we refer to our PDA for our long-range plans more than we consult with God about them.

The problems of spiritual arrogance have transcended the centuries. And the prescription given by James that was applicable in the first century is equally relevant in the twenty-first.

Chapter 10

Are Gossip and Arrogance Pulling You Down?

James 4:11-17

What's Ahead

- Stop the Slander (4:11a)
- Halt the Judging (4:11b-12)
- Don't Boast in Your Confidence (4:13-17)

*H*aving concluded the equivalent of an altar call for his readers to repent and seek reconciliation with God for their prodigal ways, James begins an extended passage (4:11–5:6) in which he deals with some specific problems in the Christian community. It is as if he has been given a diagnostic list of the sin ailments and viruses that have infected the church family, and it is now time for him to give some spiritual prescriptions.

The problems addressed in the present passage are slander, judging, and self-confidence. As we will see, each involves an outward action and an inward attitude that are inconsistent with God's principles. Thus, James writes with a "now cut that out" tone. He is not ambivalent. He labels each behavior as sin, so he fully expects his readers to bring it to a screeching halt.

Stop the Slander (4:11a)

James tells us to refrain from "speaking evil against each other." In that simple phrase, there are two important distinctions to unpack. Let's take them in reverse order:

- *"Each other"* could be interpreted universally, as in "don't speak evil against any person anywhere." That's a good principle to live by, but James probably had a narrower focus. When he says "each other," he seems to be referring to people within the church. Since he is writing his letter to church groups, and since he expected his letter would be read at a church meeting, he probably means "don't speak evil against others in the church family." This interpretation is further underscored by his reference to the readers as "dear brothers and sisters."

- *"Speak evil"* has a harsh tone to it. While the Bible often condemns gossip, James is probably talking about something more serious. Gossip involves a "behind their back" discussion of a fact or rumors, usually with an intent to make a person look bad. James is probably referring to speech that is more vindictive than gossip. He seems to be referring to slander, which involves making an intentionally false statement about someone for the express purpose of damaging his or her reputation. When you gossip, you can be telling the truth, but you are motivated to do so (consciously or subconsciously) because the incident reflects poorly on the person you're talking about. But when you slander someone, you manipulate the facts into a lie, with the specific intent to damage the person's reputation.

The Bible repeatedly condemns slander. In fact, the

Old Testament deals with slander against God or another person more than any other transgression, such as when the psalmist David speaks for God:

> *I will not tolerate people who slander their neighbors* (Psalm 101:5).

And the New Testament also characterizes slander as being despicable in God's sight, such as when Jesus said,

> *From the heart come evil thoughts, murder, adultery, all sexual immorality, theft, lying, and slander. These are what defile you* (Matthew 15:19-20).

James's readers were familiar with the denouncement of slander in their sacred texts and in the teachings of Jesus. James didn't need to explain what he meant. It was enough for him to point out that it was happening and that it should stop. End of story.

Halt the Judging (4:11b-12)

Criticism and condemnation of others are close cousins to slander, so James moves seamlessly into more discussion of these sins. Basically, he is rebuking a judgmental attitude. He isn't speaking of the type of judging that occurs at an Olympic diving competition or a photography contest; such judging involves an assessment of skill, technique, creativity, and artistry. Rather, James is telling his readers to avoid attitudes that are critical of the actions, character, and motivations of others. He is rebuking people who strut around with a superior attitude, acting as if others are less worthy while critiquing their failings and flaws.

Since James is condemning the condemning attitude of his readers, you might wonder if he is equally guilty of the condemnation he condemns. Not really. Here and throughout his letter, he does not set himself up as superior to his readers. He doesn't claim he is perfect. He doesn't flaunt his leadership role in the Jerusalem church and belittle their status. James had the humility of Paul, who despite his exemplary religious credentials, considered his accomplishments to be as valuable as garbage (Philippians 3:8). James is not disapproving of his readers as persons. He is not condemning them as individuals. In contrast, he is disapproving and condemning of *conduct* and *behavior* that violates biblical standards. He intensely cares for his readers (as demonstrated by his repeated references to "dear brothers and sisters"). He is concerned for their salvation, and he wants them to realize that continued behavior that does not reflect Christ's love may be an indication that their professed faith is a sham.

When we devalue other people, we are dishonoring people for whom Christ died on the cross. God considers them worthy enough to have His Son die for them, so we should view them with the same regard.

God's law instructs us to love each other:

> *Owe nothing to anyone—except for your obliga-*
> *tion to love one another. If you love your neighbor,*
> *you will fulfill the requirements of God's law. For*
> *the commandments say, "You must not commit*
> *adultery. You must not murder. You must not*
> *steal. You must not covet." These—and other such*
> *commandments—are all summed up in this one*
> *commandment: "Love your neighbor as yourself."*
> *Love does no wrong to others, so love fulfills the*
> *requirements of God's law* (Romans 13:8-10).

When we are judgmental and condemning of each other, and when we slander others, we are violating God's law of love. James equates such behavior with condemning the law itself. By ignoring it and disobeying it, we are disrespecting the principles God considers sacred.

A judgmental attitude also disrespects God directly. God alone is our judge. Who else can know the condition of a person's heart? When we are judgmental of others, we are haughtily elevating ourselves and usurping God's authority. James asks if we have the right to do so (a question to which the answer is obvious). Paul was a little more direct and confrontational when he addressed the problem:

> *Who are you to condemn someone else's servants? They are responsible to the Lord, so let him judge whether they are right or wrong. And with the Lord's help, they will do what is right and receive his approval* (Romans 14:4).

Does James Want Us to Be Quiet About Sin?

James wants us to be very guarded in what we say about our Christian brothers and sisters and in how we think about them. Good comments and positive thoughts are acceptable, but critical comments and disapproving opinions should be off limits. Okay, but what if you are offended by one of your Christian brothers or sisters? (Not just something trivial, like they didn't smile at you when they walked by in the parking lot. But something major, like they cheated you in a business deal or spread a bunch of lies about you for who knows what reason.) Does James expect you to just keep your mouth zipped and suck it up in these circumstances?

Although he doesn't refer to it in his epistle, James would heartily endorse the biblical process for dealing with these types of situations. Here is how Christ explained the procedure:

> *If another believer sins against you, go privately and point out the offense. If the other person listens and confesses it, you have won that person back. But if you are unsuccessful, take one or two others with you and go back again, so that everything you say may be confirmed by two or three witnesses. If the person still refuses to listen, take your case to the church* (Matthew 18:15-17).

Notice that the procedure is consistent with James's teaching in that it keeps the dispute as private as possible at the beginning. The negative repercussions are kept on a "need to know" basis as long as possible, in the hope that the problem can be dealt with privately before it is made public.

Don't Boast in Your Confidence (4:13-17)

When you are judgmental of others, you make them look smaller. You end up looking bigger—at least in your own mind. So, the judgmental person often has an inflated opinion of himself or herself. This leads to arrogance. It is bad enough when we are arrogant toward others, but it is worse when we are arrogant toward God.

James warns his readers that they may be guilty of pride and overconfidence that is affecting their reliance upon God. When we are totally convinced we are incapable of handling life, then we anxiously turn to God. But just the opposite happens when we think we have everything under control. In that scenario, we mistakenly believe we don't need God's help, because we are fully capable of dealing with any situation that may arise.

The desire of anyone with genuine faith—which James is all about—is to know and do the will of God. If we are sincere followers of Christ, we should want what He wants for us, not what we might otherwise want for ourselves. James mentioned this at the outset of his epistle:

> *If you need wisdom, ask our generous God, and he*
> *will give it to you* (1:5).

James isn't alone in emphasizing the importance of seeking to know God's will and the desire to do it:

- *David:* "I take joy in doing your will, my God, for your instructions are written on my heart" (Psalm 40:8).

- *John:* "This world is fading away, along with everything that people crave. But anyone who does what pleases God will live forever" (1 John 2:17).

- *Peter:* "If you have suffered physically for Christ, you have finished with sin. You won't spend the rest of your lives chasing your own desires, but you will be anxious to do the will of God" (1 Peter 4:1-2).

- *Jesus:* "I have come down from heaven to do the will of God who sent me, not to do my own will" (John 6:38).

James points out the blatant presumptuousness of plowing through life with no regard for God's will. He gives an example of a businessman who makes long-term plans without seeking God's direction in the process. How arrogant to presume we can know what is best for us in the long term, when we don't even know whether we'll be alive tomorrow.

God's Will About What?

James says our plans should be wrapped in prayers that seek God's will. To what extent should you apply this principle?

- Should you pray for God's will in choosing between two available parking spaces?

- Do you need to pray for God's will before you pay your household bills each month?

- Should you pray and wait for God to reveal His will when a child needs to be kept from running into the street?

- How about praying for God's will on investing money in that adult video store venture your brother-in-law is proposing?

Remember that James is a practical guy. He is not suggesting that you have to say the "if the Lords wants us to" prayer when the decision has no spiritual effect (like the parking spaces), or is obviously appropriate (the household bills), or is obviously necessary (saving a child from danger), or is blatantly inappropriate (owing a porn video store). James is directing his comments at the arrogance we display when we fail to seek God's leading in the significant decisions of our lives about which His will is not already revealed. When God's will about a choice or a plan is not obvious from what we can read in Scripture or what we know about God's character, then we should pray for His wisdom so we don't rely on our own instincts. If we intuitively think we are capable of making a wise decision on our own, then we are too arrogant and shouldn't trust our own judgment.

Planning on our own without consulting God reveals a spirit of pride and arrogance. We should abstain from such evil. Rather than boasting about our own capabilities and resources, we should approach God in humility and reverence. This gets back to the distinction between human wisdom and God's wisdom.

James knows that none of his readers can argue about this. The arrogance of asserting independence from God is patently wrong. And just to be clear about it, James reminds them that since they know decisions should be couched in God's will, then failing to do so is a sin. Again, James reveals that he is a blunt and practical guy.

■ ■ ■

Study the Word

1. How do you distinguish between *gossip, rumors, slander,* and *evil speech?*

2. Explain why God can judge us but we shouldn't judge each other. What's the difference between being judgmental and identifying sinful behavior?

3. What are some examples of life decisions we make without including God in the process? When is it not necessary to do so? When is it essential?

4. Asking God to reveal His will is easy, but discerning God's will is more difficult. How is it done?

5. Is there any connection between a judgmental attitude and a spirit of arrogance that excludes God from the planning process?

But when our nation [the Roman Republic] had become great because of toil and justice…the lust for money, and then for power overcame them…These were, I think, the root of all evils. For avarice destroyed honor and integrity…and taught instead insolence and cruelty.

—*Sallust*
(Roman historian, 86–34 BC)

The Perverted Power of Wealth

Our culture aspires to achieve wealth. For many, the motivation is greed. For a few, the drive is motivated for social good. But even the philanthropic among us bestow financial gifts out of their excess. Let's face it. Those of us who live in North America, regardless of our economic status, enjoy a lifestyle far more lavish than experienced by the majority of the rest of the world.

You might say, "Hey, it's not my fault I was born into an affluent culture instead of Third World poverty." To be sure, you had no control over the circumstances of your birth. But you do have control over the disposition of your wealth. And that is what James is getting at in this passage.

Because the excessive wealth of professional athletes, Hollywood celebrities, and business entrepreneurs is so well publicized, it would be easy for us to read through James 5:1-6 and miss a personal application (and conviction). It would be easy for us to say, "Well, this section applies to the super-rich, and that's not me." But whether we have little or lots, we have lots more than the millions around the world who have absolutely nothing. In their eyes, and in God's, we have wealth. And in that respect, the challenge made by James has personal relevance to each one of us.

Chapter 11

How's Your Sense of Social Justice?

James 5:1-6

What's Ahead

- A Sharp Warning (5:1)
- The Uselessness of Riches (5:2-3)
- Sins Against the Poor (5:4-6)

This passage stays with James's consistent theme that some people who claim faith in God don't really have it, as shown by the evidence of their lives. Here the telltale sign that exposes their disingenuous faith is the way they handle their wealth. In what is perhaps his most stinging rebuke, James condemns the way these people have hoarded their wealth and abused the poor in the process.

As you study this passage, notice how James departs from his usual writing style. In these verses he writes like the Old Testaments prophets who spoke on God's behalf in condemnation of ungodly and unjust behavior, such as when Isaiah rebukes the wealthy and their mistreatment of the poor:

> "Your houses are filled with things stolen from the poor. How dare you crush my people, grinding the faces of the poor into the dust?" demands the

> Lord, the LORD of Heaven's Armies (Isaiah 3:14-
> 15).

The Bible clearly and repeatedly underscores the dangers inherent in money and our relationship with it. Our natural sinful desires often come to fruition at the prospect of getting more of it:

> *People who long to be rich fall into temptation and*
> *are trapped by many foolish and harmful desires*
> *that plunge them into ruin and destruction. For*
> *the love of money is the root of all kinds of evil.*
> *And some people, craving money, have wandered*
> *from the true faith and pierced themselves with*
> *many sorrows* (1 Timothy 6:9-10).

The judgment that James proclaims in this passage can serve as a warning to all of us.

James Has No Problem with Money

James is not saying that money is bad. Money is not the root of all evil; rather, it is the *love* of money that causes problems. James never says that having wealth is a bad thing. His gripe is with the people who worship money more than God, who misuse money, and whose religious faith is a sham as proven by how they handle their money.

A Sharp Warning (5:1)

James begins by intentionally grabbing his readers' attention with a "Look here!" In effect, he is saying, "Hey, listen up!" This interjection serves to separate the previous passage (in which he addressed people who plan without God's input) from the present one, in which he is singling out a different group of offenders.

Although James refers to "you rich people," the context of this verse and the entire passage clearly shows he is referring specifically to the wealthy who didn't maintain a spiritual perspective with their money. Thus, we should read his reference to "you rich people" as more specifically "you *unrighteous* rich people." Furthermore, he is not talking about all unrighteous rich people—rather, his comments are directed at those who claim to be followers of Christ. These people are prime examples of what James has been preaching throughout his entire epistle. They say they are Christians, but their behavior proves otherwise.

In a prophetical future tense, James states that the wealthy will be *weeping* and *groaning*. These words were often used to convey the honest and uncontrolled emotions that accompany grief and remorse. James was saying, in other words, that tough times were going to be coming to the wealthy, and they would be crying out in pain when it appears. James is reiterating a common biblical theme— that God will eventually pour out His judgment on the unjust wealthy (later in life or at their time of eternal judgment). And their money will do them no good then:

> *What sorrows await you who are rich, for you have your only happiness now. What sorrow awaits you who are fat and prosperous now, for a time of awful hunger awaits you"* (Luke 6:24-25).

The Uselessness of Riches (5:2-3)

Prosperity can be transitory. It comes and it goes. So

if we are depending upon ourselves instead of God, we might be tempted to try and hoard wealth and possessions when they come our way. This was one of the sins of the wealthy to whom James was writing. To confront their wayward thinking, he reminds them that riches are temporal and perishable. First he mentions all of the ways in which wealth was measured during the first century, and then he identifies its vulnerability to decay:

- *"Riches"*: usually associated with agricultural production derived from landholdings. They rot away (like fruit that has spoiled).

- *"Fine clothes"*: since the wealthy wanted to be easily identified, they wore fine garments. Those fabrics get eaten by moths.

- *"Gold and silver"*: precious metals in the form of jewelry and coins. They rust and corrode. (Actually, gold and silver don't rust, but James was speaking poetically, not literally.)

These rich people concentrated on the accumulation of earthly treasure to the exclusion of heavenly treasure. James reminds them they have been hoarding these riches even though it is futile to do so. Given the perishable nature of riches, the wealthy should not be focused on "storing up" things of merely mortal significance. Instead, their focus should be on things that are valuable in God's paradigm, as Christ taught:

> *Don't store up treasures here on earth, where moths eat them and rust destroys them, and where thieves break in and steal. Store your treasures in heaven, where moths and rust do not destroy, and thieves do not break in and steal. Wherever your*

treasure is, there the desires of your heart will also be (Matthew 6:19-21).

James proclaims that such rotting riches will be the evidence that brings judgment on the rich. Much as in the grim predictions made to Ebenezer Scrooge by the Ghost of Christmas Future, James is telling these rich people to repent and change their evil ways, or else the horror of his predicted judgment will fall on them.

What If We Call It "Saving" Instead of "Hoarding"?

Can "hoarding" be rationalized as a prudent savings program? No. The problem with hoarding is that it makes money unavailable for the poor. Besides being a sign of self-reliance and greed, it prevents money from being used to benefit those who need it the most. This is the spiritual basis on which God chooses to financially bless some Christians—so they may use their money to bless others:

> God will generously provide all you need. Then you will always have everything you need and plenty left over to share with others...He will provide and increase your resources and then produce a great harvest of generosity in you. Yes, you will be enriched in every way so that you can always be generous (2 Corinthians 9:8-11).

Sins Against the Poor (5:4-6)

So far we know that James was critical of his hearers' hoarding on two accounts: 1) it showed they considered themselves independent instead of God-dependent; and 2) by hoarding their riches, they weren't making their money available to the poor. All that is bad enough, but

James is just getting warmed up. Now he blasts the rich for accumulating their wealth through economic exploitation and financial oppression.

Can there be any doubt of how James (and God) feels about this? James says the farm laborers are crying out that they have been cheated out of their pay. And to make his point even stronger, he uses the literary device of personification, saying that the wages themselves are crying out in protest. These cries have reached the ears of God Himself, and that is not a good thing for the wealthy. Thus judgment is impending as James was predicting.

The economy of the Mediterranean region was based on agriculture. Since the majority of the population was poor and uneducated, they worked as day laborers in the fields. With a glut of workers, and relatively few landowners, the law of supply and demand gave all of the bargaining power to the wealthy. The rich could delay paying wages, or withhold them entirely, and there wasn't anything the workers could do about it. But delaying the payment even one day past the day on which it was earned would work a tremendous hardship on the workers. Because they had no economic security or steady source of income, they were living hand to mouth. They needed each day's wage to buy that day's food for their family.

Recognizing the potential for abuse by the wealthy, God had instituted laws and regulations for prompt payment of workers. The wealthy landowners were certainly familiar with Old Testament rules such as...

> Do not defraud or rob your neighbor. Do not make your hired workers wait until the next day to receive their pay (Leviticus 19:13).

> Never take advantage of poor and destitute laborers, whether they are fellow Israelites or foreigners

living in your towns. You must pay them their wages each day before sunset because they are poor and are counting on it. If you don't, they might cry out to the LORD against you, and it would be counted against you as sin (Deuteronomy 24:14-15).

Remember when James wrote that it is sin when you don't do what you know you ought to do (4:17)? This is a perfect example of that principle. The wealthy knew they should be fairly treating and paying their workers, but they refused to do so. This was repeated and continual sin. Heartless conduct of this kind reveals the "dead faith" that the epistle of James is all about.

But the sins of the wealthy don't stop with their abuse of the poor working class. They were also guilty of gross indulgence. Although they wouldn't use their hoarded wealth for paying their debts to their workers, they lived an exorbitant lifestyle. Using the image of a fattened animal ready for sacrifice, James says they have stuffed themselves and are now ready for God's judgment.

The sobering conclusion to this passage refers to the death of the innocent poor, caused by the abuse and unfeeling behavior of the wealthy. The rich defrauded the workers and, as a result, the poor died unnecessarily. Through abuse of their power and their wealth, the wealthy were guilty of murderous oppression of people who were unable to defend themselves.

When James refers to God as "the Lord of Heaven's Armies" (5:4), he is using a term that emphasizes God's power and might. This indicates, in effect, that God will go to war against the wealthy in defense of the poor. Of course, maybe God's retribution won't happen during this lifetime, but there will be an accounting at the final Day of Judgment. That is when God will turn away many who professed to believe in Him:

> *Then the King will turn to those on the left and say, "Away with you, you cursed ones, into the eternal fire prepared for the devil and his demons! For I was hungry, and you didn't feed me. I was thirsty, and you didn't give me a drink. I was a stranger, and you didn't invite me into your home. I was naked, and you didn't give me clothing. I was sick and in prison, and you didn't visit me." Then they will reply, "Lord, when did we ever see you hungry or thirsty or a stranger or naked or sick or in prison, and not help you?" And he will answer, "I tell you the truth, when you refused to help the least of these my brothers and sisters, you were refusing to help me." And they will go away into eternal punishment, but the righteous will go into eternal life* (Matthew 25:41-46).

The lessons in this passage transcend the almost 2000 years since they were written. From God's perspective,

- Earthly wealth is transitory. If it is here today, it can be gone tomorrow. It is subject to the vagaries of time and the economy. Therefore, we should be making investments in matters that have eternal significance.
- Our wealth should not be built upon the oppression of others. We should be fair and just in all our financial dealings. Wealth gained through cheating is a curse.
- The wealth we may have should be used to help others. Blessings given to us by God are for the purpose of allowing us to further His kingdom.

Whatever our lifestyle, we need to examine ourselves by these standards.

■ ■ ■

Study the Word

1. Read the story of the rich man and the beggar (Lazarus) in Luke 16:19-31. What are the lessons this story has in common with those articulated by James?

2. Contemporize the passage. If James were making these points in the twenty-first century, what abuse would he criticize? What examples would he use?

3. What are some ways in which you might be guilty of excess and self-indulgence?

4. What are some practical ways in which you could assist the poor with the extra God has blessed you with?

5. What are some ways in which we can monitor ourselves to see if we are falling into the "love of money" trap?

> Jesus tells us to set our hearts on the kingdom. Setting our hearts on something involves not only our serious aspiration but also strong determination. A spiritual life requires human effort. The forces that keep pulling us back into a worry-filled life are far from easy to overcome.
>
> —*Henri Nouwen*

James Comes Full Circle

James is coming into the homestretch of his letter. He's down to the concluding paragraphs. Just 14 verses to go. And like any good author, he is going to go back to where he started as he wraps it all up.

This passage begins the final summation. It focuses on the suffering that many of his readers are enduring. Remember back at the beginning when James said that trials and troubles in life were a good thing because they strengthened our faith (1:2-4)? Well, he is back on the same issue, but this time he focuses on the need for patience and perseverance during the trials and struggles. True to form, he expects patience as proof of a sincere faith, and that says absence of patience may reveal a lack of saving faith.

Our trials may be different than those of first-century Christians. (Probably very few of us worry about being thrown to lions in an arena full of spectators.) Regardless of the differences, our struggles are no less real and oppressive to us. So the encouragement James gives to his readers should be equally pertinent to our personal situations.

Chapter 12

Can Your Patience Persevere?

James 5:7-12

*T*he focus of this section is fairly obvious. As James said at the beginning of his letter, patience during struggles is an essential part of spiritual growth. In the process, however, he makes a few new points (such as indicating we shouldn't disparage others, even though they might be the cause of our problems, and we shouldn't let our impatience and frustration be vented in our language and expressions). The passage might seem disjointed unless you recognize the *patience* theme that underlies the thoughts:

- 5:7-8—Patience is a necessity in the Christian life, and an example can be found in nature;
- 5:9—By the way, patience requires harmony or it cannot be maintained;
- 5:10-11—The prophets of old are a good example to

133

follow because they showed patience under difficult circumstances; and finally,

- 5:12—Don't let your patience break down to the point where your frustration comes out in your words, so be circumspect in what you say and how you say it.

Notice that James seems to shift a bit in regard to the people he is writing to. In the last section and previously in his epistle, he was clearly denouncing those people in the church who weren't really Christians at all (as evidenced by their fake faith, which had no goods works associated with it). In the present passage through the end of the letter, he seems to be embracing those in the churches who are sincere and authentic believers. (He goes back to referring to "dear brothers and sisters.")

Hang In There! (5:7-8)

You can't miss James's point about having patience. In a span of five verses (5:7-11), he uses the word (or a derivative of it) a total of seven times:

- Four times he uses the Greek word *makrothumeo*, which is the root word for "patience." It conveys the idea of waiting with calm and expectancy.
- Two times James uses the Greek word *hupomone*, which can be translated as "patience" or "perseverance." It suggests a sense of patient endurance and fortitude.

These two words are also paired together in Colossians 1:11, which gives a similar encouragement to what James is suggesting:

> *We also pray that you will be strengthened with his glorious power so you will have all the*

endurance [hupomone] *and patience* [mạk-
rothumeo] *you need.*

There is a little bit of "bad news/good news" in this
passage, and it has to do with how long James expects his
readers to have to be patient and endure their present sufferings. He starts with the bad news—they must be patient
until Christ returns to earth. But he is quick to add the
good news—Christ is coming back really soon.

Okay, as we mentioned earlier, scholars believe the
epistle of James was written in about AD 65. Rounding
off, that is about 1,950 years ago, and the return of Christ
hasn't happened yet. So, what is with "the coming of the
Lord is near" promise? Was James mistaken, or have we
just missed it?

Some scholars believe that James had his understanding
of Christ's timetable all messed up (they criticize his Chris-
tology and eschatology). They contend that verse 5:8
reveals an expectation of Christ's return within James's lifetime. The preponderance of scholars, however, interpret
this passage to mean that James did not intend to give an
estimated time of arrival for Christ, and they support their
position with the following arguments:

- James wouldn't place such a heavy emphasis on
  "patience" and "perseverance" if he believed that
  Christ's return was just a few days off.

- James uses the example of a farmer's patience for
  his crops. In the eastern Mediterranean region, it
  requires two seasons of rain to mature a crop. The
  farmers have to wait through both the fall rain and
  the spring rain. The way in which James writes this
  example reveals that he is emphasizing the "double"
  aspect—double rain requires double patience, but

the farmer has double confidence that the crop will reach the point of harvest.

- James would have been very familiar with the statement made by his half-brother, Jesus Christ, that the exact timing of His return was a divine secret: "No one knows the day or the hour when these things will happen, not even the angels in heaven or the Son himself. Only the Father knows" (Matthew 24:36).

The New Testament does not teach that the return of Christ is *immediate* ("just about to happen"). Rather, along with other New Testament writers, James believed that Christ's return was *imminent* ("could happen at any time," but not necessarily right away). Peter does a good job of explaining that Christ might return at any moment, but since that might not happen, in the meanwhile we should live in a holy manner for the long haul:

> *You must not forget this one thing, dear friends: A day is like a thousand years to the Lord, and a thousand years is like a day. The Lord isn't really being slow about his promise, as some people think. No, he is being patient for your sake. He does not want anyone to be destroyed, but wants everyone to repent. But the day of the Lord will come as unexpectedly as a thief...We are looking forward to the new heavens and new earth he has promised, a world filled with God's righteousness. And so, dear friends, while you are waiting for these things to happen, make every effort to be found living peaceful lives that are pure and blameless in his sight* (2 Peter 3:8-15).

Thus, Christians are told both to expect Christ's return, but also to keep living for Him until it happens. We have a split focus: We may be in the midst of suffering and tough times here on earth, but we have a view of a perfect future with Christ. The constant expectation of Christ's return is what gives us hope for the future. And that hope and confidence, like those of the farmer, can be the basis for our patience.

No Grumbling in the Meanwhile (5:9)

The reality of it all is that some of our present grief may be caused by other Christians in our local fellowship. Let's face it—some Christians can be annoying. They find fault like a reward is being offered for it. James realizes this fact, but he tells us to suck it up. He doesn't want us to fall into the trap of grumbling about each other.

James pleads this point in the context of having just referred to Christ's imminent return. He doesn't want his readers to be judged by Christ for bickering with each other. While the judgment on Christ's return will be one of eternal destiny for those who do not know Christ, believers will go through a different type of judgment. Our salvation is assured through faith in Christ Jesus, but in a type of rewards ceremony our deeds—both good and bad—will be examined and evaluated:

> On the judgment day, fire will reveal what kind of work each builder has done. The fire will show if a person's work has any value. If the work survives, that builder will receive a reward. But if the work is burned up, the builder will suffer great loss. The builder will be saved, but like someone escaping through a wall of flames (1 Corinthians 3:13-15).

James does not want us discredited at the time of judgment because we didn't have the patience to refrain from griping about the annoyances of our Christian brothers and sisters.

A Suffering Example (5:10-11)

When you think of suffering, especially suffering of biblical proportions, your thoughts might go directly to Job. He knew a thing or two about suffering. Likewise, the Jewish Christians to whom James was writing would also think back to Job and the ancient prophets in their heritage. James suggests that these prophets are examples of endurance in the face of prolonged suffering.

Unbeknownst to him, Job was at the center of a cosmic challenge between God and Satan. Satan alleged that Job was a faithful follower of God only because God had blessed him with great prosperity. God knew better, but He allowed Satan to "test" Job by intervening in the circumstances of Job's life and decimating his idyllic situation. Literally within moments, Job received news that...

- a band of desert marauders had stolen his oxen and donkeys and killed his farmhands;

- all of his sheep and shepherds had been killed in a freak firestorm;

- raiders had stolen his camels and murdered his servants;

- a fierce windstorm had caused the collapse of a house, which killed all of his sons and daughters.

Job's patience was revealed in his refusal to "curse God and die" (as his wife had recommended). He revealed a perspective on life that was the secret to his endurance of such tragedy. This perspective enabled him to worship God in the midst of adversity with the same intensity and reverence he had during times of prosperity:

*Should we accept only good things from the hand
of God and never anything bad?* (Job 2:10).

The lesson from Job and the other prophets is simply
profound, and profoundly simple: It is easy to trust God
with the oversight of our lives when we are enjoying
the ride, but we should also trust Him when the going
gets hard. Even when it gets *very* hard. And since God
brought Job through those trials and restored his prosperity (although that might not happen to everyone),
shouldn't we also have the patience to allow God to work
through the circumstances of our lives to accomplish His
will?

Like Job, we need to come into a deeper understanding
of how God works. When we appreciate that God uses difficult situations to strengthen our faith (check back to James
1:2-4), those circumstances will be easier to endure.

A Simple "Yes" or "No" Will Suffice (5:12)

This next verse (5:12) is a bit of a puzzler. James tosses
in the phrase "but most of all" (which is also interpreted
as "above all" in some translations). There is no consensus
among the commentators as to whether James is trying to
make a distinction between what he has just said (about
patience) or what he will be saying next (the power of
prayer). Because this exhortation occupies only one verse,
it seems he is making a summary statement of his discussion on patience in suffering.

What is it that James wants us to view as "most of all"?
It is the realization that we need to watch our language in
the midst of our suffering. Just as Job never verbally lashed
out, so we must also keep control of our tongue. You'll
remember that James has touched on this issue in every
other chapter of his epistle:

- 1:26—If you can't control your tongue, your religious faith is worthless.
- 2:12—Remember that you are being judged for what you say.
- 3:2-11—The tongue is a beast to control, but true Christians work diligently to do so.
- 4:11—Don't speak evil against each other.

Perhaps the exhortation in 5:12 connects with the "don't grumble about each other" from 5:9, but now James tweaks the message a little bit. He tells his readers not to take an oath. It seems that the swearing of oaths could have been a sign of impatience displayed by the poor who lived under the oppressive treatment of the wealthy. The point of the verse is that taking an oath—invoking God's name in a proclaimed statement in order to strengthen its emphasis or to underscore the truthfulness of what was being said—should be avoided. James wasn't going out on a limb here. This teaching is consistent with what Jesus taught (see Matthew 5:34-37).

There may be several reasons why James offered this instruction. Perhaps he was concerned about...

- the pagan culture's tendency to swear an oath to a pagan god in every situation; or
- the importance of maintaining high standards for our speech (such that everything we say should be truthful, so something shouldn't be considered more truthful because we attach God's name to it); or
- the avoidance of attaching God's name to a statement that is knowingly false or a promise that doesn't get fulfilled.

Whatever the reason, the encouragement seems consistent

with James's constant awareness that Christians should conduct themselves in a manner that reflects the sincerity of their faith.

■ ■ ■

Study the Word

1. Think of a time when you endured particularly difficult circumstances. Was patience a problem for you? How did you manage to persevere? Other than the problems themselves, what spiritual challenges did you face because of the experience?

2. Why is it so easy for us to grumble and complain about each other? Do we find some kind of satisfaction in doing it? Why is James so concerned about this issue?

3. Can you think of someone who has been a good role model for you when it comes to being patient during hard times?

4. Can you articulate the difference between *immediate* and *imminent* when it comes to expecting Christ's return?

5. Why are people, including Christians, often cavalier about using God's name in their expressions? How do you think God feels about this?

Three ministers were meeting together. One had symptoms of the flu, one was suffering back pain, and the other was battling arthritis. Together they read the instruction of James 5:16 to "confess your sins to each other and pray for each other so that you may be healed." They decided to give it a try. The first minister said, "I'm embarrassed to say this, but I must confess that I have a drinking problem." The second minister said, "And I must confess that I've been embezzling from the church offering." The third minister said, "I confess that I have a problem with gossip, and I can't stick around to pray because I suddenly have to make a few telephone calls."

$\mathcal{P}$rayer $\mathcal{M}$atters

Church services and most church functions are closed with a prayer. Following that tradition, it seems only logical that James will conclude his remarks with a discussion of prayer. What do you want to bet that he'll weave into his comments a reference to the "true faith has results" principle? You guessed it—a Christian who doesn't have a habit of prayer probably struggles in his or her faith, because ongoing prayer with God is evidence of a faith that is vibrant. No prayer is the equivalent of no conversation with God.

This passage is famous and a bit controversial, not because it deals with prayer, but because it discusses healing from sickness through prayer. There is a fairly significant split of opinion on this text, so watch for it.

Don't be surprised at how abruptly the epistle ends. James doesn't have any "give my regards to so-and-so," like those that pop up at the end of Paul's letters. Remember, James is too blunt for that kind of small talk. But even though his final sign-off is only two verses long, it packs a punch by summarizing his primary objective for writing his epistle in the first place.

Chapter 13

Does Your Faith Have a Prayer?

James 5:13-20

*I*f you miss the point of this passage, you aren't trying very hard to find it. It's all about prayer. In fact, except for the final two verses, James mentions prayer in every verse.

Prayer and suffering seem to go hand-in-hand. When we're buried by problems, then we're praying to God and asking for relief. Or (maybe it's "and") we're asking God, "Why me?" But since you've studied the epistle of James, you'll use your prayers to thank God for your problems because they give the opportunity for your faith to mature. Then you'll ask God for the wisdom to discern His direction throughout the difficult circumstances. (See? And you were wondering whether this epistle would have any relevance to your real life. Now don't you feel foolish!)

Watch for the variety of situations in which James says that prayer is not only appropriate, but necessary. He mentions several different circumstances. But interestingly, his verses can also be categorized by the person (or persons) who are supposed to do the praying. There is an instructive correlation between the type of circumstance, the type of prayer being offered, and the person(s) who should be saying the prayer.

The Prayer of the Individual (5:13)

James wants *you* to pray if you are suffering. The *you* part is easy to understand, but the definition of *suffering* takes a little explanation. The King James Version of the Bible uses the word *afflicted* in this verse. Since affliction has more of a physical-illness slant to it, many people have thought that the sufferings referred to in this verse mean sickness and physical infirmities. This is an understandable mistake, especially since the following verses refer more specifically to physical illness.

The concept James is addressing is prayer during times of trouble. Of course, trouble (suffering) can include physical illness, but James is suggesting something much broader. He does not specifically mean health problems. Instead, he wants us to pray in times of general distress or misfortune. Whenever you are experiencing problems of any sort, you should pray about them.

> *Give all your worries and cares to God, for he cares about you* (1 Peter 5:7).

Don't simply pray that your troubles will go away (although that request can be at the top of the list). Also ask God to give you the patience and perseverance to stay faithful during the trouble as long as He allows it to continue (remember 5:7-8?).

Thank Him for His promise to draw near to you during these tough times if you draw near to Him (4:8).

But don't pray only when times are tough. James also says you should pray when you "have reason to be thankful." Of course, we should always be thankful to God in all situations (see Ephesians 5:20), but this isn't what James is referring to. He means those times when circumstances are pleasant, or when times remain tough but we have managed to spiritually transcend the difficulties through our trust in the Lord.

Make Your Prayer Life Balanced

Try devoting equal time in your prayers to requests for relief from the problems and praises to God for His faithfulness and the hope you have in Him. Prayer requests and praises of thankfulness are integrally related:

Don't worry about anything; instead, pray about everything. Tell God what you need, and thank him for all he has done. Then you will experience God's peace, which exceeds anything we can understand. His peace will guard your hearts and minds as you live in Christ Jesus (Philippians 4:6-7).

The Prayer of the Elders (5:14-15)

After mentioning prayers during rough circumstances and smooth times, James moves to the specific circumstance of sickness. In this situation, you are of course supposed to be praying for yourself. But James doesn't mention that. Instead, he limits his discussion to prayers on your behalf by the elders of your church.

There were "elders" in the Jewish synagogues during Christ's earthly ministry, but by the time James was writing his letter, the first-century churches had been established long enough for his readers to recognize that this reference to "elders" meant the leaders in the local Christian church. Notice that James uses the plural term *elders*. The New Testament contemplates that church leadership is always a group undertaking; it is never vested solely in just one individual. This plural reference also makes it clear that James was not referring to a person who might be a faith healer. If there is going to be a miraculous healing, there will not be any credit given to any single individual. God doesn't want one person to go about boasting that he or she "has the power." Credit should go to God, and that is more likely to happen if the prayers are offered by a group of dedicated Christian servants who have devoted themselves to the spiritual care, leading, and protection of the church family.

Don't skip over James's instruction for the sick person to initiate the call for the elders. There is humility required when someone asks for help. That is part of the attitude God wants us to have when we go into prayer.

What's the Deal with the Oil?

James says that the elders should anoint the sick person with oil as they pray. There is debate among scholars as to whether the anointing is symbolic and ceremonial (like the many anointing rituals in Old Testament times) or whether it is intended to be medicinal (such as when the Good Samaritan put oil on the wounds of the victim he aided). Maybe it doesn't really matter, since James clearly indicates that the healing will not come from the oil. The closing of verse 15 reveals that "the Lord will make [the sick person] well."

James makes a bold and affirmative statement that God will heal the person in conjunction with a "prayer offered in faith" by the elders. This statement is puzzling to scholars because this passage is the only one in the New Testament epistles that deals directly with the issue of physical healing. And you always have to be careful when you build a theology around a single verse. What makes this passage even more intriguing is the fact that James makes an unconditional statement: The prayer of faith *will* result in the sick person being healed. That sounds like a pretty good guarantee—one that could put the entire medical profession out of business. (Pity the poor drug companies.) The questions raised by scholars include...

- Does James really mean *physical* healing? Perhaps he intends a more metaphysical reference—to the person's *spiritual* healing.

- What is the basis on which God heals? Is it the faith of the elders, the faith of the sick person, or something else?

- Is this an infallible procedure that happens all of the time, every time? If so, what is going wrong when the sick person is not healed?

- Is sin somehow involved with the illness (which might block the anticipated healing)? James makes a reference to forgiveness of sin in 5:15.

- Is James speaking for his time only? Many people believe that miraculous events, such as healings, were reserved for "the apostolic age" (that early period of Christianity's first few decades, when miracles were used to help prove the authority and truth of the gospel message being preached by Peter, Paul, and the other apostles).

If some of these distinctions were intended, it seems strange that James didn't mention them. Since he spoke without restriction or limitation, it appears that the crucial puzzle piece is the definition of "the prayer offered in faith." Of course, no mature Christian would doubt God's power and ability to heal a sick person, so every prayer by elders offered for a sick person will include faith in God's ability to heal. And the person who is ill will have accompanying faith (both in God's ability and in the confidence that the healing will happen).

But James is apparently suggesting a level of faith beyond mere confidence in God's ability to answer. He is referring to a prayer, offered by the elders, in which they have the absolute conviction that it is God's sovereign will that this particular sick person will be healed. (This kind of faith—knowing for sure the parameters of God's will in a specific situation—is a spiritual gift, as mentioned in 1 Corinthians 12:9. God gives these gifts as He chooses, so not everyone has this gift of supernatural faith that discerns God's actual will.) So, the restoration of health will naturally follow only when it is God's will to do the healing. And the "prayer offered in faith" is, therefore, merely an advance acknowledgement that in His sovereignty, God will heal this particular person on this particular occasion.

With this understanding of the passage, we must also realize that...

- God still wants the elders praying, even if none of them senses the specific spiritual gift of faith that accompanies the promised healing. Their prayers are not wasted. God may still choose to intervene in response to the prayers of His people.

- God doesn't heal on every occasion, regardless of how earnestly people pray. Sometimes, it is simply not His will for the person's health to be restored. In such situations, we must trust in His love and His wisdom. (And this gets us back to "when troubles come your way, consider it an opportunity for great joy" and "if you need wisdom, ask our generous God, and he will give it to you" of 1:2-4.)

Although James makes a reference to sin, he doesn't indicate that sickness is always associated with sin. Sometimes it is (see Mark 2:1-12); sometimes it isn't (see John 9:2-3). Sometimes it is God's will for us to struggle continually with an affliction (see 2 Corinthians 12:7-10). The significance and meaning of this reference may be revealed in its connection to the promised healing to a prayer offered in faith. In such situations, *if* sin was a factor in the illness, it will be forgiven in the process.

The Prayer of Friends (5:16a)

James enumerates several principles about prayer throughout this passage, including that God responds to prayer and God forgives sins confessed in prayer. Consequently, James instructs us to be praying for each other in times of sickness. This is more than just an "Oh, by the way, God, please help Stan get over his gastrointestinal peculiarities." Honest prayer with our Christian brothers and sisters requires authenticity and honesty, and this involves confession of sins. We need to put things on the table with God and get honest with Him. Getting honest with each other is part of the process.

The Prayer of the Righteous (5:16b-18)

James has no doubt that our prayers can be effective in bringing about amazing results. He boils it down to this equation:

- If a person who is righteous before God (the kind of person who has the vibrant faith that produces Christlike behavior)...

- prays earnestly and honestly to God...

- the prayer will be effective (evoking God's response, drawing us to Him, even if God gives us an answer that is different than what we're hoping for).

If your prayers seem weak and ineffectual, it may be due to the fact that your faith is weak and ineffectual. A mature faith prays with the ultimate and underlying request that God's perfect will be done in our lives, whether or not His will is aligned with our preferences.

As an example of a righteous man and the results that follow his earnest prayer, James points to Elijah. So that his readers wouldn't say, "Well, I could never be like the prophet Elijah," James notes that Elijah was a human just like us. He was not uniquely gifted, but he was a man known to have a heart for God, which allowed him to know God's heart.

This About Sums It Up (5:19-20)

In typical blunt fashion, James concludes his letter in just two verses. But also in typical fashion, James doesn't miss the opportunity to reiterate his theme one more time. Note the components of his theme, articulated in a fresh way:

- *The one who wanders away*—this may be a person who momentarily turns from God, or a person who thinks himself or herself to be a Christian but has dead faith and is not a Christian at all.

- *The fate that awaits them*—for the person who has wandered away from God, the disconnection from

God is a form of death; but for the nonbeliever, his or her eternal death is in view.

- *The ones who can help*—each of us is instrumental in restoring or bringing the wanderers to life with Christ. We play an integral role in the restoration process.

- *The goal of salvation*—for the rebellious Christians, their wayward spirits are reformed and they come back into fellowship with God; for the fake Christians who professed faith but never had it, they will—for the first time—come into the realization of God's presence and grace with the forgiveness of their sins.

Unlike his evangelistic appeal in 4:7-10, which was made to those who were not genuine believers, James is signing off his letter with a call to authentic Christians to be diligent in their responsibilities to those who are lost. As followers of Christ, the best thing we can do is to reflect His love. We project the character of Christ only when we are growing in our faith and showing God's love and kindness through our speech and actions. James wants it no other way.

◼ ◼ ◼

Study the Word

1. Can there be benefits for us to pray, even when God doesn't give us what we are asking for?

2. Have you been praying for anyone who is struggling with severe health challenges (perhaps yourself)? Describe the nature of the faith with which you pray. Do you agree there can be a special type of faith that actually knows for sure the will of God?

3. Explain what you think might be the relationship between prayer and confession of our sins.

4. Give your definition for what it means to be a righteous person who prays earnestly. What are the results? Does this person always receive what is being asked for?

5. What is James trying to say in the last two verses of his epistle? If there were only one thing you could remember after studying his epistle, what would he want it to be? By the way, what is the one thing you'll remember the most?

Dig Deeper

$\mathcal{W}$e like to write, but we really like to study. As with all of our books, the writing of this Bible study was preceded by many hours of study and research. We've come across many books that we found quite helpful and informative. Hoping that you'll want to proceed further in your study of James, we'd like to recommend the below-listed books to you.

Commentaries

A great verse-by-verse commentary is the Life Application Bible Commentary New Testament Set. This series covers the entire New Testament, but there is a single volume on the epistle of James. If you want practical application, this is a good place to start. The commentary was written by the same team that designed and wrote the notes to *The Life Application Bible.*

William Barclay wrote an excellent commentary set in The Daily Study Bible Series. From his New Testament Commentary series, you can select a single volume that covers James (along with 1 and 2 Peter). He takes a passage at a time (usually about 10 to 15 verses) and gives great background information to the text.

Our very good buddy Jon Courson has a readable New Testament commentary, not surprisingly called *Jon Courson's Application Commentary—New Testament*. Jon's preaching style is very casual and very relevant to everyday life, and his commentary is written in a similar style.

Perhaps the easiest resource to read is the Thru the Bible Commentary Series. This set was taken from the *Thru the Bible* radio broadcasts of Dr. J. Vernon McGee. Nobody says it plainer than Dr. McGee. There is a hardbound set that covers the entire Bible (James is in the volume that covers 1 Corinthians through Revelation), but you can also purchase a single paperback volume, *James*.

If you like going into detail, check out John MacArthur's volume on James from his MacArthur New Testament Commentary.

Another commentary set is the Tyndale New Testament Commentaries. There is a separate volume for James that was written by Douglas J. Moo.

Also on our list is the James volume of The NIV Application Commentary, written by David P. Nystrom.

General Bible Study Helps

We don't have enough modesty to keep us from mentioning our own *Knowing God 101* and *Knowing the Bible 101*, which are part of the Christianity 101 series.

We're always pulling *A Survey of the New Testament* by Dr. Robert H. Gundry off the shelf for background information.

Another one of our favorite Bible scholars is Dr. Lawrence O. Richards. His *Bible Teacher's Commentary* is excellent.

There is an Old Testament volume and a New Testament volume for *The Bible Knowledge Commentary* (John F. Walvoord and Roy B. Zuck, general editors). These books will take you verse by verse through the entire Bible.

Bible Translations

Lots of translations of the Bible are available to you. We suggest that your primary study Bible be a *literal* translation (as opposed to a paraphrase), such as the *New International Version* (NIV) of the Bible, or *The New American Standard Bible* (NASB). However, it's perfectly acceptable to use a Bible paraphrase, such as *The Living Bible* or *The Message,* in your *devotional* reading.

The translation we used in this study on James is the *New Living Translation* (NLT), a Bible translation that uses a method called "dynamic equivalence." This means that the scholars who translated the Bible from the original languages (Hebrew and Greek) used a "thought-for-thought" translation philosophy rather than a "word-for-word" approach. In the final analysis, the Bible that's best for you is the Bible you enjoy reading because you can understand it.

A Word About Personal Pronouns

When we write, we prefer to capitalize all the personal pronouns that refer to God, Jesus, and the Holy Spirit. These would include *He, Him, His,* and *Himself.* However, not all writers follow this practice, and there's nothing wrong with that. In fact, personal pronouns for God were not capitalized in the original languages, which is why you'll find that many English Bible translations use *he, him, his,* and *himself.*

Download a Deeper Experience

Bruce and Stan are part of a faith-based online community called ConversantLife.com. At this Web site, people engage their faith in entertainment, creative arts, science and technology, global concerns, and other culturally relevant topics. While you're reading this book, or after you have finished reading, go to www.conversantlife.com/101 and use these icons to read and download additional Christianity 101 material from Bruce and Stan:

 Resources: Download study guide materials for personal devotions or a small-group Bible study.

 Videos: Click on this icon for interviews and video clips on various topics.

 Blogs: Read through blogs and articles and comment on them.

 Podcasts: Stream ConversantLife.com podcasts and audio clips.

conversant life .com

engage your faith

Christianity 101®

Now That You're a Christian

If you're a new believer, you'll connect with these honest, encouraging responses to questions that new Christians often have. You'll discover what God has done for humanity, how you can know Him better, and how you can reflect the love of Christ to people around you.

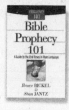

Bible Prophecy 101

In their contemporary, down-to-earth way, Bruce and Stan present the Bible's answers to your end-times questions. You will appreciate their helpful explanations of the rapture, the tribulation, the millennium, Christ's second coming, and other important topics.

Creation and Evolution 101

In their distinctive, easy-to-access style, Bruce Bickel and Stan Jantz explore the essentials of creation and evolution and offer fascinating evidence of God's hand at work. Perfect for individual or group use.

Knowing the Bible 101

Enrich your interaction with Scripture with this user-friendly guide, which shows you the Bible's story line and how each book fits into the whole. Learn about the Bible's themes, terms, and culture, and find out how you can apply the truths of every book of the Bible to your own life.

Knowing God 101

Whatever your background, you will be inspired by these helpful descriptions of God's nature, personality, and activities. You will also find straightforward responses to the essential questions about God.

Bible Answers to Life's Big Questions

In response to the many questions they've received, Bruce and Stan tackle some of the biggest issues about life and living the Christian faith, including, What happens when we die? Is Christ the only way to salvation? How can we know there is a God? Is the Bible true?

Growing as a Christian 101

In this fresh look at the essentials of the Christian walk, Bruce Bickel and Stan Jantz offer you the encouragement you need to continue making steady progress in your spiritual life.

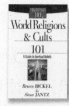

World Religions and Cults 101

This study features key teachings of each religion, quick-glance belief charts, biographies of leaders, and study questions. You will discover the characteristics of cults and how each religion compares to Christianity.

Christianity 101® Bible Studies

Genesis: Discovering God's Answers to Life's Ultimate Questions

"In the beginning" says it all. Genesis sets the stage for the drama of human history. This guide gives you a good start and makes sure you don't get lost along the way.

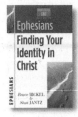

Ephesians: Finding Your Identity in Christ

Verse for verse, the book of Ephesians is one of the most profound, powerful, and practical books in the Bible. This guide reveals the heart of Paul's teaching on who believers are in Christ.

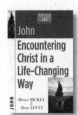

John: Encountering Christ in a Life-Changing Way

This study reveals who Jesus is by demonstrating the dramatic changes He made in the lives of the people He met, including Nicodemus, the woman at the well, Lazarus, and John, "the disciple whom Jesus loved."

Philippians/Colossians: Experiencing the Joy of Knowing Christ

This new 13-week study of two of Paul's most intimate letters will inspire you to know Christ more intimately and maintain your passion and vision. Filled with helpful background information, up-to-date applications, and penetrating, open-ended questions.

Acts: Living in the Power of the Holy Spirit

Bruce and Stan offer a straightforward look at the ongoing ministry of Jesus through the church. They highlight the drama of the early Christians' triumph over darkness and their explosive growth from a band of 120 fearful followers to a thriving, worldwide church.

Galatians: Walking in God's Grace

The apostle Paul blows the lid off fake, "rules-added" Christianity and describes life in God's Spirit, through His grace—which is still God's way of freeing you to live out your full potential as His child.

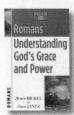

Romans: Understanding God's Grace and Power

Paul's letter to the church in Rome is his clearest explanation and application of the good news. This fresh study of Romans assures you that the Gospel is God's answer to every human need.

James: Working Out Your Faith

James is bursting with no-nonsense guidance to help you grow in practical ways, including perceiving God's will, maintaining a proper perspective on wealth and poverty, and demonstrating true wisdom in your speech and actions.

1 & 2 Corinthians: Finding Your Unique Place in God's Plan

This enlightening study explores the apostle Paul's helpful responses to issues that churches continue to face today: maintaining unity in the church, exercising spiritual gifts, and identifying authentic Christian ministry.

Revelation: Unlocking the Mysteries of the End Times

Have you ever read the final chapters of the Scriptures, only to finish with more questions than answers? Bruce and Stan help you understand Revelation's encouraging message and apply it to your life today.